Here's what peo
The S

"Stephen's approach to teach... ... ... wisdom is helping to prepare them for the workforce. As a business owner, I am surprised how little financial understanding there is amongst my younger employees. Having young people understand the financial system makes them better employees."
-Paul Picton, President, Maverick Chocolate Co.

"Financial literacy is so important for youth today. Understanding how to be fiscally responsible, safely move money, pay for goods and services, and save for the future is so key as they enter adulthood. *The Seed Tree* helps prepare today's youth and I thank Stephen for his commitment to our young adults and tomorrow's future leaders!"
-Steve Max, Executive Vice President, U.S. Bank

"For all the great things we do to build innovative critical thinkers, somehow we never prepare students for something as basic as how to manage their finances. So to have Stephen Carter, one of the most engaging and inspiring teachers I know, write a book to help young people think about money and finances is educational gold!"
-Dr. Dean Nicholas, Head of School, Cincinnati Hills Christian Academy

"I am so grateful that Stephen Carter has chosen to invest his time and energy into writing *The Seed Tree*. It's never too early to start imparting this knowledge to the next generation and I couldn't be more proud of the organization that Stephen has build around scaling this training to young people everywhere!"
-R. Scott Collins, Chairman and CEO, Link-age

THE SEED TREE

A Financial Fable

Money Management and
Wealth Building Lessons for Teens

Stephen Carter

ISBN: 978-0-578-98319-6

For Vernon,
My grandfather and mentor

Want to Start Building Wealth?

Looking to become the master of your money?

Visit the Seed Tree Group (www.seedtreegroup.com) to learn about our engaging online classes (including a free sample class) and resources designed to help you achieve a lifetime of wealth and happiness.

Your journey to financial freedom starts today. Grab your phone and take a picture of this QR code to get a coupon for 30% off the purchase price of any class.

At The Seed Tree Group (www.seedtreegroup.com) we're committed to helping you take control of your finances and take charge of your life.

Sign up today.

Contents

INTRODUCTION

When I first started teaching, I knew everything. The wisdom of a twenty-three-year-old, after all, is surpassed only by his extensive experience in life, and I was prepared to share all of this life knowledge with the high school students I hoped to positively influence.

"Every hour," I would say, "should be a reminder that we will never get it back, that once it is spent, it is gone forever."

I would then pull up the famous line from Rudyard Kipling's poem "If": "If you can fill the unforgiving minute."

The lecture would continue by examining Kipling's choice of the word *unforgiving* and considering what was implied by its usage. We would talk of great figures from the past who were now gone, and we would consider ourselves twenty or thirty years into the future and imagine who and what we would be.

It was, overall, a fun exercise. And, year after year after year, as students filed in and out of my classroom and therefore in and out of my life, I continued to preach the importance of savoring every hour.

And here I am, fifteen years later. My first classes of students are now in their early thirties and they are established in their careers and families. Many of them come back to visit, sometimes to make me feel old, and sometimes to reminisce about those discussions way back when.

"You know, Mr. Carter," they say, "you were right when you said how fast time goes. I feel like I was just here, walking these halls."

"You want to talk about time going fast," I say. "How do you think it makes me feel to see a thirty-two-year-old who a few years ago was sitting in my class at age sixteen?"

The passing of time has made me realize even more how precious of a commodity it is. Strangely, it is also the most easily squandered, and thus I have doubled down on my efforts to convey to my students the necessity of making the most of one's time.

Perhaps the most striking example of the power of time comes from its application to money. Ask the average adult when he or she started investing and taking the concept of growing wealth seriously and most will say "not early enough." That's typical for most of us—we learn these concepts well into our careers and after we have lost the gift of the most powerful compound interest earning years of all.

Consider the following example—if an individual begins saving $200 a month for retirement at age twenty-six, she would have just over $1 million by age sixty-five. If that same individual started ten years earlier, at age sixteen, she would have $2.8 million by age sixty-five. The numbers speak for themselves.

The question then became, "How do I convey these concepts to those who can make the biggest difference in their financial lives armed with this knowledge?" I began searching for just the right book to teach these principles and impress upon teens the urgency of acquiring financial literacy early. I quickly ran into a roadblock: while most of the best-selling books by the financial gurus have a "for teens" or "for kids" version, those versions tend to be watered down and patronizing, and if there's one thing that teenagers hate, it's someone talking down to them.

While there are some well-written, helpful books to teach personal finance skills to young adults, those books tend to be dry and boring in their approach. And the only thing worse than being watered down and patronizing is being boring.

Thus, my frustration.

The solution, it seemed, was to write my own personal finance guide for people who are just starting on the path to adulthood and who, ultimately, are at a crossroads, whether they know it or not. The decisions made in high school and in college regarding money will establish a path that can lead either toward financial freedom and happiness or toward financial ruin and debt.

It is true that these skills are still not regularly taught in schools. School is great for teaching us how to land a career but fails in instructing us how to manage the money that career will bring. The school of hard knocks can certainly be a valuable teacher in many areas of life, but when it comes to money, it doesn't pay to miss out on the power of time, which truly is our greatest asset. Armed with the skills of financial literacy, young adults can make decisions that, because of the time value of money, will reap benefits for the rest of their lives.

That's the WHY behind The Seed Tree Group, a business dedicated to teaching financial literacy to young adults through online classes and resources that aid in one's quest toward wealth and happiness. Feel free to email me directly (Stephen@seedtreegroup.com) as I love hearing from my readers.

Regarding this book's format, rather than just compile a list of financial principles, I decided to tell a story—the fable format is one of my favorites because lessons always go down easier when accompanied by characters and a plot. So, as you read about Andrew, a high-school sophomore, and his classes with Mr. Sharp, please understand that the ultimate goal is to come away more knowledgeable about managing money. And, if you enjoy the story along the way, that's just an added bonus.

Best of luck,
Stephen Carter
www.seedtreegroup.com

THE SEED TREE

A Financial Fable

Seed tree, *noun, "a tree that bears seed, specifically, a tree left uncut to provide seed for forest reproduction"*
—Merriam-Webster

CHAPTER ONE
THE INCENTIVE

There is, in fact, a year of high school that transcends the other years. Not, of course, the first year of high school where the student, a deer-in-the-headlights freshman, wanders the halls of academia in a constant stupor. Nor is it the third year where the student, a brain-fried-beyond-recognition junior, is burned out from AP exams and college applications. While most would assume it is the senior year, that one is also off the list because the persistent, gnawing desire to leave high school clouds all other experiences. No, the best year of high school is the second one—unburdened by the frustrations of ninth grade yet not forced into cynicism by the required college focus of eleventh and twelfth grade, the sophomore views the world as his oyster. Or, if not an oyster, then at least a little less frustrating than the other three years (aside from the usual headaches over homework, extracurriculars, and finding a significant other—or at least the prospect of securing a temporary one before the homecoming dance). Such was the case for Andrew Black, who was a few days away from being officially declared a tenth-grade student.

It also meant that it was time for him to sit down with his guidance counselor, Mr. Lantz, in order to plan out his schedule for the upcoming year. Andrew was joined by his friend Kevin, a fellow soon-to-be-sophomore. After signing up for geometry, microeconomics, American literature, and chemistry, Mr. Lantz displayed the list of elective offerings. The list was extensive to say the least—covering everything ranging from The Art of War and Horticulture Management to Science Fiction Lit and Photography. After some hesitation, Kevin pointed to The Art of War and looked at Andrew expectedly.

"Let's take this one," he said. "Sounds cool and from what I hear, it's a pretty easy class without much work."

"Looks good," Andrew said, "but my parents wanted me to talk about it with them before I finalized my classes."

"I'm doing Art of War," Kevin said to Mr. Lantz. "Am I good to go?"

He handed his form to the counselor, who nodded and said, "Good to go."

"Coming?" Kevin asked.

"You go ahead," said Andrew. "I'm going to look over the options again."

"Suit yourself," Kevin said, grabbing his backpack and heading for the door. "I'll save you a seat at lunch."

With that, Kevin left the office, leaving Andrew to puzzle over his partially completed form.

"Do you have any questions about the classes, Andrew?" asked Mr. Lantz.

"I was curious about this one," Andrew said, pointing to a class at the bottom of the list.

"Ah, Developing Financial Intelligence," said Mr. Lantz, "now that's an interesting choice. Not actually being taught by one of our teachers—this is an outside person who is coming in to offer this class. His name is Mr. Sharp. He stopped by our office a few weeks ago and asked if we had a personal finance for teens class and when I said no, he offered to teach one. Administration checked him out and he seems legit so he's coming in once or twice a week to teach this class. Not much interest from anyone else, though. The class only has four students signed up."

"Does that mean I shouldn't do it?" asked Andrew.

"No, not necessarily, just means you'll have a small class, that's all. Plenty of time for discussion, I'm sure. Look, he left this handout if you want to look at it. Feel free to take it with you and let me know what you decide."

"Thanks, I will," said Andrew, taking the handout as he got up to leave.

"You know, Andrew," Mr. Lantz said as Andrew reached the door, "if there was one thing I wished I had learned in high school, it would have been money management. School teaches you a lot, but it sure doesn't teach you how to handle your money."

"Yeah, you sound a lot like my dad right now," Andrew said.

"Ha—well, he sounds like a smart man, your dad. All I know is that I could have avoided quite a few mistakes had I taken a class like this one. Take care."

It wasn't until later that night, after dinner, that Andrew remembered the handout Mr. Lantz had given him. He fished it out of his backpack and unfolded it on the kitchen table to look over the information. The inside was dotted with charts and graphs along with phrases like "compound interest" and "build your wealth" in large font. The longer Andrew stared at it, the less appealing the class sounded overall.

"How did scheduling go?" Andrew's mother asked as she placed the last remaining dishes into the sink.

"Pretty easy," Andrew said. "Just have to make a decision about my elective."

"What's that you're looking at?" Andrew's father had walked up behind him and was now peering intently over his shoulder.

"It's this new class the school is offering—it's one of the elective options and I thought it sounded interesting. Or at least I thought you would think it sounded interesting," Andrew said, smiling up at his father.

"Well I like the name—Developing Financial Intelligence. That's one area where I think the school does a disservice to the students—not teaching them about money."

"My guidance counselor said the same thing," said Andrew, "and I told him he sounded like a broken record of you."

"I'll keep saying it until the school starts teaching it," said his father.

"Sounds like they're teaching it now, honey," said Andrew's mother.

"Are you going to take it?" Andrew's father asked.

"I don't know—honestly, it sounds pretty boring. And only four other students are in it. Kevin's taking The Art of War and that sounds a lot cooler."

"Who's teaching The Art of War?"

"Mr. Swanson. It's supposed to be pretty easy. Kind of a blow-off class."

"A 'blow-off class,' huh? Well, that's not exactly ideal. Both are a semester long?"

"Yes," said Andrew, "just one semester. And I'm already taking a few hard classes, so one easy one wouldn't hurt too much."

"No, it wouldn't," said his father. "However, the opportunity to take a class that will directly impact your future is something not to pass up. I'll tell you what, I'll make you a deal."

"A deal?" asked Andrew.

"If you take this class, and if you listen and do all the work and get an A, I'll give you a financial incentive."

Andrew perked up.

"What kind of financial incentive?" he asked.

"When you complete the class to my satisfaction," said his father, "I'll give you $1,000."

"Wait! Seriously?" Andrew said, more loudly than he planned.

"John, you can't be serious?" asked Andrew's mother.

"I'm totally serious," said Andrew's father. "One thousand dollars if you take this class and report regularly to me regarding what you are learning and how you are implementing it."

"So just to be clear—I get $1,000 for taking the class and completing it to your satisfaction? Like you'll just give me $1,000?" Andrew asked, looking up at his father in disbelief.

"Yes—that's how strongly I believe in you learning these concepts. Your mother and I constantly say that if we had learned financial skills in high school, the entire trajectory of our lives would have been different. Don't get me wrong; we're not exactly living in poverty here, but we made so many mistakes starting out that have just recently become apparent to us. I don't want the same for you."

"Well, yes, OK, sure, I'll take the class. And I have to get an A?"

"You have to listen and do all the work and then get an A. You have to take it seriously. You have to listen to your instructor and take good notes and then debrief with me after each class."

"I feel like you keep adding things to this deal," Andrew said, frowning up at his father.

"And you have to write a five-page essay that—"

"Ha—whatever. Now I know you're full of it," Andrew said.

"OK, so that last one was a joke but, seriously, take the class and pay attention. I do want to hear what you are learning, and I do want you to apply the principles. And if you do all that, the $1,000 is yours to spend however you want."

"Deal," Andrew said as the two shook hands.

CHAPTER TWO
CLASS BEGINS

The next day Andrew took his course option sheet by Mr. Lantz's office and left it on his desk. And, just like that, with a simple designation on a sheet of paper, the trajectory of his next school year was set in motion. The summer flew by, as summers often do, and the students found themselves entering the school building in mid-August with the goal of locating the classes now arranged on their schedules.

"I see you signed up for Accounting for People Who Hate Fun, or whatever it's called,"

Kevin said, elbowing Andrew in the ribs. "I'll look forward to hearing all about it while I coast through mine. I heard, from a reliable source, that Mr. Swanson rarely even makes students show up for his class."

"Yeah, well, I have my reasons for taking the finance class," Andrew said, deciding to keep his father's incentive quiet for the time being.

The sophomore elective period was at the end of the day so Kevin and Andrew parted ways at 1:35 p.m. to head to their respective classes. Andrew's schedule designated room 205 for Developing Financial Intelligence and when he arrived, he found himself in a large classroom with a conference table in the center that had five chairs arranged around it. Three of the chairs were already occupied—two with silent students Andrew recognized as juniors, and one with a man who appeared to be in his early or mid-forties with a gray-speckled beard and a pen stuck behind his right ear.

"Welcome!" said the man, standing to his feet. "You must be Andrew."

"I am," Andrew said, heading toward one of the empty chairs.

"I was expecting you," the man said. "And now, it seems, we are ready to start. We had two students drop at the last minute so there will just be four of us."

At these words the two juniors looked at each other and exchanged wide-eyed glances before one of them spoke up.

"Uh, Mr., um," she said.

"Mr. Sharp," the man said, smiling at the girl. "You can call me Mr. Sharp."

"Um, Mr. Sharp, um I think, well, we, I mean Cynthia and I, well, we are supposed to meet with Mr. Lantz this bell, I believe."

"Well, I wouldn't want to keep you," said Mr. Sharp, gesturing to the door.

The two juniors grabbed their binders and hurried out of

the door letting it slam behind them.

"Andrew," said Mr. Sharp, "I'm not one to prophesy, but I'd venture to guess that this class just got smaller by two students. How do you feel about a one-on-one class?"

"Uh," said Andrew, "Fine, I guess."

"Excellent," said Mr. Sharp. "Then let's get started. Andrew, I'd like to get to know you, and I'd also like to tell you about myself. Who do you want to start?"

"You can start," said Andrew.

"My name is Philip Sharp, and I'm what's called an account services manager at a business called Thomas Jacobson. I also run a small financial advisor agency with just a handful of clients, and I specialize in getting out of debt and building wealth. Let's see, what else? I'm married; I have two children—my younger is a junior in high school and my older daughter is about to graduate from college. I have two dogs, I love to cook, and I enjoy backpacking through the woods. That about sums it up—your turn."

"OK, well, I'm Andrew Black, I'm fifteen and I'm a sophomore."

"You can do better than that," said Mr. Sharp. "When do you turn sixteen?"

"November," said Andrew.

"Are you looking forward to getting your license?"

"Yes, absolutely," said Andrew.

"And what do you do in your free time?"

"Like besides school?"

"Besides school. Do you play any sports? What are your hobbies or pastimes?"

"I run cross country," said Andrew. "And I am really into movies."

"Any specific ones?" asked Mr. Sharp.

"Older ones. Definitely *not* superhero ones. Dramas mostly, but also some comedy. Not horror or anything."

"I'm a bit of a movie buff myself," said Mr. Sharp. "How about siblings?"

"Nope, I'm an only child."

"OK, well, Andrew, it's a pleasure to meet you. You're enrolled in Developing Financial Intelligence. What do you suppose this class will be about?"

"Is that a trick question?" Andrew asked.

"Nope—genuinely interested."

"Money, probably," said Andrew. "Like how to manage it and how to not get in debt. Things like that."

"You're certainly on the right track," said Mr. Sharp. "This is a semester-long class which, according to the school calendar I was just given, means that it ends toward the beginning of December. I should also tell you up front that I'll not be giving you a final exam."

"Really?" asked Andrew. "No final? Sweet."

"No final exam—if, by December, you don't know the material then I failed in my job of teaching it."

"Sounds good to me," said Andrew.

"Well, in that case, I suppose we should jump right in."

And start they did. Mr. Sharp dove immediately into the difference between checking and savings accounts and how each one worked and why it was necessary to have both. Before long, Andrew's head was swimming with information and his notebook was covered with mostly illegible scribbling.

"Am I going too fast for you?" asked Mr. Sharp.

"No, I'm just, well, I'm fine."

"Information not that interesting?" asked Mr. Sharp, smiling.

"No, it's not that, I mean, it's just that, well, isn't this all just kind of basic? Like doesn't everyone know what a checking account is and how a savings account works? My parents opened a savings account for me when I was seven and that's where my birthday check from my grandparents always goes."

"Ha!" Mr. Sharp laughed and sat down across from Andrew. "Yes, in fact, it is basic. But you'd be surprised how many people don't know these things. Many students don't even open a checking account on their own until they graduate from college and by then they are thousands of dollars in debt and in a hole so deep they'll spend most of their twenties digging themselves out.

"Understanding the basics is key to creating a strong foundation for your financial life. Your checking account is like the Grand Central Station for your finances. Your money, or income, comes in and goes into the account. Then it gets funneled into all sorts of trains, some for spending, like a budget that we'll discuss at some point, and some for saving, like your savings account. Your checking account is constantly being rebalanced based on the money coming in and the money going out while your savings account just has money coming in, no withdrawals, at least not regularly.

"Understanding how each work and function is key. But before we drive that home anymore, let's try a different start," Mr. Sharp continued, "Tell me, Andrew, what is it you hope to do in life?"

"Do in life?"

"In other words, where do you see yourself fifteen years from now?"

"Fifteen years from now. I haven't really thought about that before. I'd be thirty years old. I guess I'll be working in business or something," Andrew said. "I don't know."

He paused and flipped through his notebook absently while Mr. Sharp waited in silence.

"I know I'm supposed to do something I'm passionate about, which I imagine is what you're going to say next," said Andrew without making eye contact. "But that's the thing— I mean, I like cross country and I guess I like most of my classes and I was in the school play last year, but there's nothing that I'm, like, you know, super pumped about doing."

"Andrew," said Mr. Sharp, standing up and walking to the whiteboard, "you've just revealed one of the greatest problems with having to plan for your future at your age."

With this, Mr. Sharp drew a large question mark and circled it. "You just don't know. And why should you? All you've ever known up to this point has been school and extracurriculars. I assume you have yet to complete an internship of any kind?"

Andrew shook his head.

"How many jobs have you had so far?"

"Well, none," Andrew said. "I mean other than doing some stuff around the house for money."

"That's my point," said Mr. Sharp, drawing one line off the question mark and writing "school" and "sports." "How can you expect to know what you want to do with your life if your experience has been limited to just these areas? Andrew, this is the whole point of this class."

"I thought the class was about finances."

"It is about finances and money, but money is just the means to help you accomplish what you want in life. It is really about gaining direction and understanding how to find your purpose. You have to have a starting point and although the information I talked about today was, as you said, 'basic,' it is important and none of it can happen without having established the first step."

"Which is?" asked Andrew.

"Earning an income. Getting a job. Applying for something. Working. The first step to any kind of financial intelligence is creating a source of income."

"Like, after college?"

"No, like right now. In fact, this is your first assignment—you need to go find a job. Any job will do. Don't feel like you have to find one that is a perfect fit for your passions or something that will look good on a resume. Just walk right into a fast-food restaurant and ask for an application. Or head to the nearest mall and walk up and down the main section asking if anyone is hiring. I guarantee you someone is, and I guarantee you that you won't have to look too hard. Our next class is Thursday. I want you to show up for class having secured a job."

"Ha," said Andrew, laughing nervously. "I thought you were serious for a second there."

"I'm as serious as can be," said Mr. Sharp.

"But, Mr. Sharp," said Andrew, "I'm not even sixteen. No one will hire me."

"Sure they will," said Mr. Sharp. "Plenty of places hire fourteen- and fifteen-year-olds. You'll just need a work permit, which just involves a trip to the guidance office, and I'm sure Mr. Lantz can help you with that. In fact, you can head over to talk with him right now."

Andrew put his notebook in his bag and got up to leave.

"Oh, and Andrew?" Mr. Sharp asked.

"Yes?"

"Promise me that you won't ask Mr. Lantz to let you drop the class?"

"I promise—besides, my dad really wants me to take this class."

"Well, tell your father that I said he is a wise man."

"I will. Thank you," said Andrew as he left the room.

That evening, after dinner, Andrew recalled the primary details from the day's lesson to his father in a half-hearted manner.

"Checking and saving accounts," said Andrew's father. "Anything else?"

"I'm supposed to get a job," Andrew said.

"You're supposed to get a job?" Andrew's father repeated.

"Yeah—and he was serious. He really hammered home the idea of establishing an income. Said it was the first step to financial intelligence. Kind of made me think. I mean, I have an allowance and all—"

"All twenty dollars a week of it," said Andrew's father, smiling.

"Yeah, well I guess I got to thinking that getting a job would mean that I would have more money and all. I don't know—I hadn't really thought about getting a job until after high school, but I suppose it couldn't hurt to consider getting one earlier," said Andrew.

"No, it couldn't," said Andrew's father. "And it would probably help build some character. I think it's a great idea. And I don't know if you've noticed, but just about every store you go into these days has a Now Hiring sign posted near its entrance."

"So, if I do get a job, how would I get there? I don't even drive yet," said Andrew.

"I'm sure in the meantime your mother and I could figure out a way to get you to and from work. We'd be honored to be your personal taxi service if it meant you were going to start down the road of financial independence."

"OK, well maybe I'll start looking around," said Andrew. "After all, I need to have one by Thursday. First assignment of the class."

"Sounds like you'd better get these plates cleaned up so we can drive around and get you some applications."

CHAPTER THREE
STARTING A BUDGET

Several days and multiple applications later, Andrew promptly opened the door to classroom 205 at 1:35 p.m.

"Andrew!" Mr. Sharp said, turning from the whiteboard he was in the process of cleaning. "Good to see you. I was just getting set up in here for our discussion."

Andrew came in and sat down at the large table while Mr. Sharp pulled a few books and pads of paper from his bag.

"So, Andrew, I trust you have some exciting news for me?"

"About?" Andrew asked.

"Did you complete the assignment I gave you?"

"I did, actually. Meet the newest employee of The Twist at Central Mall—the soft pretzel stand."

"I'm pleased to meet you, Mr. Newest Employee," said Mr. Sharp. "When do you start—or did you already?"

"My first day is Saturday. I'm supposed to go in for an orientation training before the mall opens, and then I get trained on the front register during the first shift."

"Sounds like a plan. How does it feel to be officially employed?"

"Good, I guess," said Andrew. "The money will be nice. They're paying me twelve dollars an hour. My dad says it's crazy because his first job paid five dollars an hour."

"Ah, yes, times have certainly changed. Well, if you're going to be bringing in all that money, we'd better get this class started."

Mr. Sharp wrote "BUDGET" in large letters on the whiteboard.

"You're familiar with a budget, I assume?" he asked.

"Yes, that's how you organize your money. My parents have one that they work on each month," said Andrew.

"Excellent. Well, next to getting an income, this is probably the most important lesson of the class: how to establish and stick with a budget. Budgets are a lot like New Year's resolutions—have you ever made a New Year's resolution, Andrew?"

"Yes, every year."

"How many resolutions have you kept longer than two months?"

Andrew smiled in response.

"That's what I thought. Welcome to the club—do you know why keeping resolutions is so hard to do?"

Andrew shrugged.

"It's because resolutions reflect a desire to change something, but they rarely or never include a means or a plan to do the changing. A lot of people resolve to lose weight so they join a gym, but after a month or so their typical habits and routines win out and they stop going, and the year rolls around and then they make the same resolution again. Changes in habit are hard and they take time and dedication. Budgets are the same—it is one thing to sit down and design a budget, but it is another thing to stick to the budget. But those who stick to the budget discover the great paradox at the center of budgeting."

"Paradox," Andrew said, sitting up, "that's one of our SAT words from English. A paradox is a contradiction that is actually true."

"Well said," said Mr. Sharp. "The great paradox of budgeting is this: It is only within the confines of the budget that a person can escape being financially trapped. In other words, they must be bound by the budget to experience freedom. Seems like a contradiction, but it is true. Pure and simple, a budget is a way for you to track the money that is coming in and the money that is going out. With the budget, your job is to make sure that you are never in a situation where more money is going out than is coming in. The money coming in is the income, while the money going out qualifies as expenses. Let's use a real-world example—you said you will make twelve dollars an hour at your new job?"

"Yes," said Andrew.

"That's pretty good," said Mr. Sharp. "Maybe I should apply there as well. How many hours are they going to give you a week?"

"About fifteen depending on the week."

"So," said Mr. Sharp, turning to the whiteboard to do some calculations, "that means that in a week you will make $180, which turns into $780 a month."

"Wow," said Andrew, perking up, "that's not bad."

"Not bad at all," said Mr. Sharp. "But don't get too excited yet—we haven't taken out taxes yet."

"But I thought I didn't have to pay taxes because I was under eighteen?"

"Partially true," said Mr. Sharp. "If you make less than a certain amount, currently $12,200, then no, you don't technically have to pay federal taxes, but they may still be withheld from your paycheck. When you file your taxes at the end of the year, you'll be able to get most or all of it back."

"Wait, file taxes? What? This sounds like it is more trouble than it's worth," said Andrew.

"Hold on now, let me explain. You'll be subject to federal and state withholding along with social security. You'll get most or all of your federal and state back at tax time, but you have to plan your budget assuming this money is gone. Your $780 is actually closer to $660 after taxes."

Andrew's smile faded.

"Hey, it's not all that bad—$660 is a lot better than you were making with your allowance, right? By the way, how much is that allowance? Are you still getting it?"

"It's twenty a week, and I get it as long as I help out around the house."

"Perfect, so we can add $86 to your monthly budget—$20 a week is $1,040 a year and that divided by twelve months is $86.66 so your monthly take-home pay is now $746." Mr. Sharp wrote this number at the top of the whiteboard.

"Now," he continued, "let's talk about your expenses. I'm guessing they are low right now considering you live at home. Is there anything you pay for yourself?"

"My dad makes me pay for my part of the cell phone bill," Andrew said. "I have to fork out over sixty dollars a month of my allowance, which is basically all of it."

"Cell phone bill," Mr. Sharp said, writing on the board, "sixty dollars. Anything else?"

"No," Andrew said.

"Think really hard because we want to consider everything when it comes to the budget. Any other regular expenses you have?"

"No, not really. I mean my parents bought me a Netflix subscription for my birthday last year and it is about to expire in a few months, and they said if I wanted to keep it I would have to pay for it, so I guess there's that. It's like fourteen dollars a month."

"And are you wanting to keep it?"

"Yes, for sure—too many good shows to pass up."

Mr. Sharp added "Netflix –$14" to the board. "Now, Andrew, how many times a month are you asking your parents if you can borrow money? What are those expenses?"

"I don't know, only a few times. I mean my dad usually gives me money when I go to hang out with Kevin at the mall, or if I want to go see a movie."

"Typically, the best way to figure out your expenses is to track them for a while. Here's what we are going to do, Andrew—we're going to embark on a research project. I want you to spend some time this week talking with your parents about their budget. Ask them to show it to you and ask them to explain to you how they track it. Then I want you to create a budget for yourself thinking through all the expenses you have on a monthly basis. When we meet back next week, I want to see a list of expenses you foresee as being part of your budget."

"OK, sounds good," Andrew said, getting up to leave.

"Oh, and hey," Mr. Sharp said, "good luck on Saturday!"

"Thanks," said Andrew.

The next few days passed in a wild blur for Andrew—Friday was the first home football game of the year and Kevin's parents invited Andrew out for pizza afterward, so he wasn't home until 10 p.m., making his 7 a.m. alarm a rude awakening Saturday morning. The first day at The Twist was a huge stress-filled event full of burning his fingers on hot soft pretzels while getting frazzled during customer orders. He spent the rest of the weekend catching up on Netflix shows and Instagram and putting off schoolwork until Sunday evening. It was then that he saw his note to devise a budget.

"Dad?" Andrew asked, "you and Mom have a budget, right?"

"We do, why do you ask? Wait, actually, let me guess—is this for your finance class?"

"Yes, I'm supposed to talk with you about your budget. Mr. Sharp's going to have me create one."

"I do like this Mr. Sharp guy," Andrew's father said. "Maybe I should be paying him the thousand dollars."

"Real funny, Dad," Andrew said.

"I'm more than happy to sit down and show you our budget if you can let me finish cleaning up the kitchen first. Wait, what am I saying? How about giving me a hand here?"

After Andrew and his father cleaned up the kitchen, they headed upstairs to the family office and Andrew's father turned on the computer and pulled up a spreadsheet with a variety of tabs lining the bottom.

"The first thing to know about a budget," said Andrew's father in a mock-professorial voice, "is that you can't spend what you don't have."

"Thanks, Dad," Andrew said, assuming a look of annoyance.

"Seriously, though, it's great that you are learning about budgets. Your mother and I did not budget for the first three years of our marriage and our finances were a disaster. Neither of us had learned the first thing about managing money and we just figured that if we were getting paychecks and didn't go crazy on spending, things would be fine. We couldn't have been further from the truth. It got so bad at one point that we had $17,000 in credit card debt, no savings, leftover student loan debt, two car payments, and a house we couldn't afford. We were a complete mess until the class saved us."

"What class?" Andrew asked, genuinely listening. He had only heard small bits of this story before, but never this much honesty about his parents' financial lives.

"A seminar class, actually. We got an email announcing thirty dollars off this Saturday class about money smarts—I still remember the advertisement: 'Want to Get Out of Debt and Get Your Life on Track? Attend the MoneySmart Seminar to Learn How to Start Today!' Ha—seems like a lifetime ago, but it was probably the best money I ever spent. It helped your mother and me turn our financial lives around, and just in time, too, because you came along soon after that."

"How did you get out of all that debt and everything? I mean, we're not in debt now, are we?" Andrew asked.

"No, the only debt your mother and I have is the mortgage and that will be paid off in another five years. We have an emergency savings fund, a good retirement account set up, some money set aside for your college, and a balanced budget. Speaking of a balanced budget"—Andrew's father shifted his attention back to the spreadsheet—"the first lesson is don't—"

"I know, I know," Andrew said, rolling his eyes, "Don't spend what you don't have. You've only said that to me one million times."

"Well then let's make it one million and one—don't spend what you don't have. Number one rule in my book."

"Mr. Sharp's number one rule is getting a job—he says if you don't have an income, then you have nothing to work with."

"And he's not wrong—the rules work hand in hand. If you're not making money, you have no business spending money. The point of a budget is to help you keep track of your spending so you don't end up spending more than you are making. Now see, here's what we've got—first are the recurring bills we must pay each month. Here's the mortgage, the insurance—we combine our car, house, and life—payment, the utility bills like water and electric, and the services, which includes trash, Internet, and cell phones. The next column here is for categories of spending—the entertainment, the eating out, the groceries, the clothing, the dog—"

"Wait, you guys have a category for Charlie?" Andrew asked, laughing.

"Yes, well he needs to eat too, doesn't he? And he has to go to the vet twice a year, and get his shots, and take his heartworm medicine. There's a lot to consider with a budget, and Charlie is included in ours. When you make a budget, you need to think about all your expenses and that includes all family members, even four-legged ones. The next column after spending is our savings column. This is the one I'm most proud of—we save over 20 percent of our total income."

Andrew's father paused for dramatic effect but seeing the blank look on his son's face, he continued. "Most people save little to nothing but the going thought is that you should strive to save 10 percent. Had your mother and I saved 10 percent from the beginning, we would be in a different place now, but we are playing catch-up for lost time, so we save double the recommended amount. Some goes into our retirement accounts, some goes into a fund for your college, some goes into an emergency fund, and some goes into our investment account. But every month we set this money aside and watch it grow—you'd be shocked at how quickly you can accumulate a sizable amount when you do it month after month."

"Well, I don't know exactly what Mr. Sharp wanted me to do with your budget. It's not like I pay for things like the mortgage or utility bills. I told him that the only thing I have to pay for is the cell phone bill, but he wants me to make a budget anyway."

"Trust me, he has a reason. If there's one thing I've learned, it's that money without a budget is basically lost already. It'll be gone faster than you can say Charlie. Speaking of Charlie, where is that dog?"

Andrew went to his room and got out a piece of paper. At the top he wrote "Budget" and then he listed "cell phone" and "Netflix." Then, just for fun, he started making a list of things he would put into a budget of his own. The list included "new clothes of MY choosing," "snowboard," "season pass to The Falls ski club," and many more things. By the time Andrew finished, he saw that his dream budget would need a lot more money than $746 a month. "Oh well," he thought, "I guess I'll see what Mr. Sharp has to say." With that, he was drifting off to sleep.

CHAPTER FOUR
NEEDS AND WANTS

"Show me what you've got," Mr. Sharp said as soon as Andrew walked in the door.

"What, no 'Hi, how are you?' or 'How was your first day of work?' or anything?" Andrew said, sensing that he could let his guard down a bit around Mr. Sharp.

"Nope, none of that gibberish, we are getting down to business—today marks the beginning of your financial future."

"I thought that happened when I first stepped foot in here," Andrew said.

"Well, yes, that's true, but today you become a man with a budget, and that is something impressive to behold."

"Fair enough," Andrew said, pulling his assignment out of his binder. "Here you go."

Mr. Sharp looked over the list on the half-crumpled piece of paper and shook his head.

"Nope," he said, "this is not going to work. What you have here is a list of wishful purchases, not a budget. Let's start with this." He grabbed a marker and drew a large circle on the whiteboard. "Know what this is?"

"A circle?" Andrew said, smiling.

"Close but not quite. This is a pie. And not just any pie— this is your budget pie. Now it will look different at every stage of your life but since you are living at home and have relatively small monthly expenses, we're going to create a budget based around where you are now. And I'm going to divide it into three sections."

Mr. Sharp drew a line down the center of the circle and then a line separating one half into two additional sections.

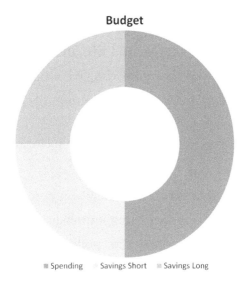

Budget

■ Spending   Savings Short   ■ Savings Long

"Your first budget pie," said Mr. Sharp, "has three components—one component makes up half, one makes up a quarter, and the other makes up the remaining quarter. The big half is your spending—this is where you can buy your new clothes, your entertainment, your eating out, and your cell phone and Netflix. This section is money that you can spend each month however you choose. You've earned it and now you get to spend it."

Mr. Sharp drew a line out to the side of the half circle and wrote the number "$373." Then he drew a line out to the side of each smaller half and wrote "$186.50" by each one. "These pieces," he said, pointing to the smaller halves, "these are for your savings."

"Both of them?" asked Andrew skeptically.

"One of them is long-term savings and the other is short-term savings. For our purposes, let's say that short term is anything between now and high school graduation. Long term would be anything after high school graduation into adulthood. An example of a short-term savings would be for a car—you are going to want a car, right?"

"Yes, true," Andrew said.

"And I'm assuming you have to pay for it yourself?"

"Unfortunately, yes," Andrew said.

"So that's a short-term goal—unless, of course, you don't need a car until college?"

"No, I'll need one well before then. Hopefully, later this year," Andrew said.

"Exactly," said Mr. Sharp. "Now we begin the hard talk."

He turned to the board and to the side of the budget pie he wrote, in large letters, "NEED" and "WANT."

"Tell me the difference," he said, pointing to the words. "What's the difference between a need and a want?"

"Well, a need is something that you have to have, and a want is something that you just, you know, want. Like something you don't really need but it would just be nice to have."

"That definition works for me. Now let's look over your spending list so far. Can you identify any needs?"

Andrew looked over his list. He paused briefly at "snowboard" and "Netflix" and then, after a moment, said, "I guess cell phone bill."

"Do you *need* your cell phone?" Mr. Sharp asked.

"Is that ... is that a joke?" Andrew asked.

"Fair enough—we can put that in the need category. Anything else?"

"I guess not really. I mean I was going to say Netflix, but I don't really have to have that."

"Did you look over your parents' budget like I asked?"

Andrew nodded.

"Did you see any needs on their list?"

Andrew thought before responding. "The bills—they had mortgage bills, insurance bills, utility bills, things like that. And groceries and clothes and things for the family. And our dog."

"Ah, the family dog," said Mr. Sharp smiling. "Always a key part of the budget. OK, so your parents have quite a few needs in their budget, but they also are running a household while you are a fifteen-year-old sophomore student in high school, so you're in slightly different places. For now, let's accept that you have few needs in your budget but mostly wants. The reason I wanted you to start thinking about this is because understanding the difference between a need and a want can mean the difference between a balanced budget and an overdrawn budget. Has there ever been a purchase you've made where you've thought, afterward, 'That was a waste of money'?"

"Sure," said Andrew. "Last month I went to a movie with Kevin and my dad didn't give me any money, so I used my allowance money to buy the ticket. The movie was stupid and a complete joke—mostly because the director apparently quit halfway through, and the studio finished the movie with another director who had a different vision and it ruined the whole thing. And it cost me thirteen dollars of my own money."

"And how did that feel at the time?"

"Super frustrating," said Andrew. "That was thirteen dollars I could have spent in so many better ways."

"Well, we all have those purchases, but the important thing is that we learn a lesson from them. There's certainly nothing wrong with going to a movie and hanging out with friends, but when it comes to deciding how we are going to spend our hard-earned money, that makes us think twice. That's why having a job is so important—once you get a job, you can view every purchase from the lens of your time. You said you make twelve dollars an hour, right?" asked Mr. Sharp.

"Yes, but it's more like ten dollars after taxes," Andrew said.

"Aha! A quick learner," said Mr. Sharp. "OK, so you make ten dollars an hour. Now if you divide that out it means that you earn one dollar for every six minutes of your time. Apply that to your spending. You said the movie was twelve dollars. Did you buy any popcorn? A drink?"

"A large popcorn and a coke; it cost nine dollars—almost as much as the movie."

"So, you spent a total of twenty-one dollars at the movie theater. If you make one dollar every six minutes, then you have to work a total of two hours and six minutes to earn the twenty-one dollars."

"What? That's crazy—that's almost as long as the movie."

"Exactly, it *is* crazy. And what's even crazier is that now you know that you'll think of every future purchase through the lens of how much it is costing you in time. And of all the resources we have, time is perhaps the most precious. When it runs out, it is gone forever."

"Dang, Mr. Sharp, way to get all dark and everything," Andrew said.

"I'm sorry. I get a bit carried away with that lesson. But that's why I'm so adamant about getting people to start budgeting. When they throw away their money, they are basically throwing away their lives—the money that has been paid in exchange for their minutes and hours and days. When you get to be my age, you think a little harder in terms of how much your time is worth."

"So, every time I buy something, I am basically spending my time," said Andrew. "One dollar for six minutes of work. I guess that does make me think twice."

"A deterrent to frivolous spending—you'll not buy so many things impulsively if you think through how long you had to work to earn the money you are about to spend."

"Fair enough, Mr. Sharp, but to get back to the budget," Andrew said, pointing to the whiteboard, "how come I have to save 50 percent of my income? My dad showed me his budget and he is only saving 20 percent."

"Your parents are saving 20 percent of their income each month? Wow," said Mr. Sharp, "I'm impressed. That's better than almost anyone I know."

"My dad said that most people are told to save 10 percent, but he had to save extra to catch up from some mistakes they made early on."

"It's true that most people will tell you to save 10 percent, but that's a concept that's been around for ages and the truth is, we live in a society where so many things are unknown. The future is changing so rapidly, and industries are collapsing while new industries rise to take their place. I don't want to get bogged down in a discussion of economics, but suffice to say, one can never go wrong with increasing savings. You're in a different situation since you live at home with your parents. Because of that, you can afford to save quite a bit more than most people—you're not paying rent or anything so you can be saving that to help you buy a car or, eventually, even a house."

"A house? Seriously?"

"Sure, why not?" asked Mr. Sharp. "If you follow the plans I'm going to give you, you'll be able to put a down payment on a house before you turn twenty-seven years old."

"You're kidding!" Andrew said, "My parents didn't even buy a house until they were close to forty. How am I going to buy one at twenty-seven?"

"Well, I'm getting a bit ahead of myself—that's material we will cover in a later lesson. For today, let's focus on finishing your budget. As I said last class, the primary purpose of a budget is to keep you from spending money you don't have."

"My dad reiterated that quite a few times last night," Andrew said.

"Yes, I definitely like your father," Mr. Sharp said. "Look at it like this. If you are getting a regular paycheck and you just assume you have money in your account and you start spending, a little here, a little there, then soon the money is gone. Some people just assume that they can keep spending and make up for it with the next paycheck. Before they know it, they are one, two, or three paychecks behind, and they are starting to rack up some serious debt. Debt is like quicksand—the more you struggle, the more it piles up; the more it piles up, the more it weighs you down until finally you feel like you can't breathe. It's not cool. What is cool is tracking your spending and keeping it within your budget. If you have $373 to work with each month, then that is your limit and you cannot, under any circumstance, go over that. Make sense?"

Andrew nodded in agreement.

"Good. Now we've got our pie filled out, so let's talk about where we are going to put these categories. Do you remember our first class where we talked about checking and savings accounts, and you said it was 'basic' information?"

"Maybe," Andrew said, smiling.

"You said that your parents had a savings account opened for you. Do you remember which bank?"

"Yeah, it was Chase or something."

"Perfect," said Mr. Sharp. "So, you have an account at Chase. That's great—most banks offer some sort of incentive when you open a checking account, and Chase is currently running a special where if you open a checking account and set up a direct deposit and deposit at least $500 in the first three months, they will give you a free $200."

"Seriously? $200? Just for opening the account?"

"Completely serious. Here's the flyer," Mr. Sharp said, handing the piece of paper to Andrew. "That's your next assignment—I want you to go to the bank with one of your parents and open a custodial account. They'll be listed on the account with you, but it will be your account. Then go to your manager at The Twist and ask for a direct deposit form. Your parents can help you fill it out."

"Just to clarify," asked Andrew, "what is direct deposit?"

"Direct deposit," said Mr. Sharp, "is a method where your paycheck gets deposited into your bank account on payday without you having to do anything. Instead of getting an actual physical check, you get a deposit that shows up on the day you get paid. In fact, and here's the cool thing, you can have it split into two payments, 50 percent each, with one going into your checking and one going into your savings. This will keep that savings safe while you can spend what is left in your checking account. We can get into the details later about how to separate your savings into long term and short term but focus on opening the account and setting up direct deposit for now."

"OK, sounds good, so just open the account, set up direct deposit, and then have half of the paycheck go into each account?" Andrew asked as he finished writing down the assignment.

"That's it."

"Sounds good," Andrew said, packing up to leave.

"You know, I'm not going to let you leave until you tell me how work was," said Mr. Sharp.

"Work was fine. Kind of crazy, but I guess I like it OK."

"What do they have you doing?"

"Working the register and bagging the hot pretzels to order. I'm not allowed to make the pretzels until I turn sixteen, so I'm just working the front of the house."

"Well, everyone has to start somewhere. Looking forward to hearing more about it. Now get out of here before I make you late to your next class," said Mr. Sharp.

Andrew barreled out of the classroom door and directly into Kevin who was just walking up the hallway.

"Watch it, dude," Kevin said, giving Andrew a small punch in the ribs. "Not all of us are so engrossed in our class that we miss the bell. Hey, how is your little one-on-one sesh with Mr. Scissors going?" he asked, laughing.

Andrew pushed Kevin to the side and laughed back. "It's Mr. Sharp to you, and it's probably a lot better than Fart of War or whatever it is you decided to take."

"Yeah, well, we spent today watching *300* so I've got you beat there. Mr. Swanson is letting us watch all the famous war movies during the class so next week we are watching *Saving Private Ryan* and *Platoon*. It's like the best class ever."

At the sound of that, Andrew felt a slight twinge of regret that he was missing out on some of his favorite movies, but he remembered the promise of the $1,000 and shrugged his shoulders.

"Hey, you want to hang out tonight and start binging the new season of *Thrashers*?" Kevin asked.

"I would, but I have to work tonight," Andrew said.

"Oh, I forgot, Mr. Working Man. It's cool, have fun with your pretzels. Maybe I'll swing by and score a free one?"

"Ha," Andrew laughed, "if it doesn't get me fired."

CHAPTER FIVE
COMPOUND INTEREST

The next day that class rolled around, Andrew headed for room 205 with a copy of his direct deposit form in hand. He and his father had set up a checking account online, applied for the $200 credit, and filled out the necessary forms from his work to set everything up. Andrew was now in his second official week at his new job, and he was already getting into a comfortable rhythm with the flow of customers and the pace of the pretzels. He was also in a good flow with his classes, although he was surprised to find, as he went to open the door, that this class with Mr. Sharp had surpassed even English as his current favorite.

"Welcome, my good sir!" Mr. Sharp jumped up from his seat and went to turn off the classroom light. "You'll want to sit right down; we have a special presentation today."

"Presentation? I hope I wasn't supposed to—"

"Nonsense, don't fret, just have a seat." Mr. Sharp went to press a button on his computer and within seconds, a colorful game show lit up the overhead screen. "Today we watch one of my favorite shows—*Who Wants to Be a Millionaire?*"

"Uh, what?" Andrew asked.

"You've seen this show before, right?"

"No—never gotten it recommended to me on Netflix."

"Ah, I forgot, Mr. Sophisticated here with his Netflix programming. Well, you are in for a treat. Allow me to explain: There are a series of contestants and if chosen, the contestant answers a series of questions on a quest to eventually make a million dollars. The contestant can cash out at any point or use a series of helpful aids to answer the question and, if answered correctly, earn more money until eventually having a shot at $1 million."

"Sounds thrilling," Andrew said with a noticeable lack of enthusiasm.

"It is, it absolutely is. Watch," said Mr. Sharp as he pressed the play button.

For the next forty-five minutes, Andrew and Mr. Sharp watched in silence as three contestants each attempted to make a run at a million dollars. Despite his best efforts, Andrew found himself getting drawn more and more into the show. When it was over and the last contestant left with just $5,000, Mr. Sharp turned the lights back on.

"Well?" he asked, looking at Andrew.

"Well fine—it was fine. I guess I enjoyed it. But what was the point?"

"So glad you asked. You tell me, does the show make it look easy?"

"Sort of, I mean, I probably could have done better than the second two, easily. Or at least made better decisions throughout. Like I would have walked when I got to $30,000 instead of missing such a stupid question."

"How many millionaires do you know, Andrew? Personally, how many?"

Andrew thought for a moment. "I don't know, I mean, Sam's parents are pretty rich, but I don't know if they are millionaires. I guess I don't really know any."

"Does the show make it look easy to get a million dollars?"

"Well, yeah, I mean, anyone can do it."

"Exactly—that's the appeal of the show. Presumably anyone can get on and, through luck and a little effort, walk away with a million dollars. It's basically the American dream on a fast track—why work hard and save your whole life when you can go on a game show and win it all in one night?"

"Now you're talking, Mr. Sharp," Andrew said, smiling. "I think that sounds like a good plan. Maybe I should put the saving categories in my budget toward lottery tickets."

"I think you get the point," said Mr. Sharp, laughing. "Becoming a millionaire is not easy. It certainly doesn't happen to many people, and it certainly doesn't happen in one night. It takes time and dedication and effort. Not to mention lots and lots of saving. There's a famous book called *The Millionaire Next Door* and the whole premise of the book is that the typical millionaire does not actually go around flaunting their wealth. The typical millionaire got to be a millionaire by living a frugal life—not spending frivolously or wasting a bunch of money on clothes and cars and houses. The people you see doing that usually are not actually millionaires, just big spenders. There's a difference, you know. A person can make $350,000 a year and not actually be rich, especially if they don't save it and work to build wealth. Let me ask you, Andrew, have you ever thought about being a millionaire?"

"Well sure, I mean, doesn't everybody want to be a millionaire? I just figured that it only happened to a few lucky people like the ones on the show."

"That's where society has led you astray, Andrew. Believe it or not, anybody can be a millionaire. All it takes is applying the principles I'm going to teach you and sticking with them."

"Are you a millionaire?" Andrew immediately regretted asking this and was about to issue an apology when Mr. Sharp responded.

"I don't particularly like to make this public but yes, I am. I'm forty-five years old and my net worth reached one million a few years ago. I don't make an incredible amount of money each year, but I have saved and invested and saved and invested since I was your age. But only because someone took the time, when I was fifteen years old, to teach me the principles I'm now teaching you."

"So, you teaching me this is sort of like a pay it forward kind of thing?"

"Something like that, yes. I always told myself that once I got to the point in my career where I could afford the time to teach, I would share my knowledge on these topics with young people in high school. There are so many things you can do as a high school student that will set you up financially for the rest of your life. But I'm getting ahead of myself. Let me ask you this, Andrew—when do you hope to become a millionaire?"

"When? Like an age? I don't know; I guess I never thought about it like that. I just assumed I would find a job and do all the life stuff and someday have some money."

"And that's how most people think, and not just people your age—most adults, even. Everyone wants to be rich, but not many people have a plan or system to get there. What if I told you, Andrew, that with a straightforward plan that doesn't require an incredible amount of savings, you could be a millionaire by the time you turn forty-nine?"

"Sounds good to me," Andrew said.

"First, let me give you a little background," said Mr. Sharp.

Mr. Sharp turned to the whiteboard and drew a picture of a tree. Underneath, he wrote "seed tree."

"Have you ever heard of a seed tree, Andrew?" he asked.

Andrew shook his head.

"I hadn't either until a few years ago when I was driving back from Florida, and I was going through a section of North Carolina. I was passing all these wonderful forests and thinking about how I wanted to stop the car and do some hiking when suddenly, I came to this barren area where a crew had just finished cutting all the trees. The cut trees were scattered over the ground and it looked like some futuristic postapocalyptic world. The thing that got me, though, was seeing just a few trees, scattered around the area, uncut. There they were, still standing, in the midst of a sea of stumps. I don't know why, but it bothered me at first—I was thinking, 'Why didn't they just go ahead and cut them all? I mean, why leave any if they are going to devastate the whole forest like that?'"

"Why did they leave them?" Andrew asked.

"Like I said, it got me, and I researched it a bit when I got home. Turns out, those few trees left standing are called 'seed trees.' After the foresters do what's called 'clear-cutting,' they leave a few trees that are strong and healthy to reproduce and repopulate the forest. Those are the 'seed trees.'"

"So, they left the trees to help grow more trees?"

"Yes, that's the plan. The seed trees would generate the seeds that would spread throughout the field to bring about a whole new crop of seed. One single tree can generate hundreds of new trees. It got me thinking—I'm a huge fan of metaphors, and the seed tree struck me as a metaphor for how money works. Think about the budget plan we came up with. All the income comes in and then between the short-term savings and the spending, three-quarters of it is wiped out in a relatively short time. What's left, the long-term savings, is like the seed tree—it grows and prospers and repopulates using a beautiful technique called compound interest."

"I know compound interest," Andrew said. "It's when your money earns more money."

"That's it in a nutshell," said Mr. Sharp. "Now let's look at what happens to your own seed tree in your budget. Currently, in long-term savings, you are saving $186 a month. Let's call it an even $200. Now, you mentioned that you had some money you were given for birthday presents saved up. How much do you have?"

"$800," Andrew said.

"And how about the $1,000 you're going to get?" Mr. Sharp asked, smiling.

"Hey, how do you know about that?" Andrew asked in shock.

"Let's just say that your father and I had a chance to meet, and all the secrets are out."

"Well, that $1,000 was supposed to help me buy a car," Andrew said defensively.

"And I'm not saying it can't," Mr. Sharp said. "But just for the sake of argument, let's say you have $1,800 to invest." He went over to the whiteboard and wrote "$1,800" at the top. "You are going to contribute $200 a month to your account. Now, let's talk about the rate of return. When you put your money in a savings account, you can expect to—"

"I know; I actually looked this up last night. My savings

account pays 0.50 percent interest a year. Apparently that's good for a savings account."

"Good for a savings account, yes," said Mr. Sharp. "But not good at all for an investment account. In an investment account, you are essentially saying that you are willing to accept more risk in order to have the potential of getting higher returns. A savings account has little to no risk—the interest it earns is a lot lower than you might get from investing, but you don't have to worry about losing the money. When you invest, the value can go up or down, depending on the type of investment and the level of risk. Typically, the higher the rate of return, the greater the risk, and the greater the risk, the greater the volatility and the chance that you'll lose money in the short run. But that's what makes this plan so great—you're not in this for the short run. You're looking at a long-term investment, which makes you able to handle some risk.

"There are a lot of different numbers I could give you to run these projections, but to make things easier, I'm going to use 10 percent as a projected rate of return for our investment. Later, I'll explain how I arrived at this number, but for now, let's do some math. Do you have a calculator by chance?"

Andrew pulled out his phone.

"OK, $200 a month is $2,400 a year. Multiply that by 1.10. What do you get?"

"It comes to $2,640," Andrew said.

"Great, now, tell me, how can you determine how long

until that becomes a million dollars?"

"Uh, do I just divide a million by 2,640?"

"Try it and let me know what you get."

"It says 378.78," Andrew said. "Wait, does that mean it would take 378 years to get to a million dollars? I'd be dead!"

"You and me both. And probably your children and your grandchildren and your great grandchildren and so on. Luckily for us, that's where compound interest comes into play. In fact, it's probably the most interesting concept in the entire world of finance."

"I assume it speeds up the process?" Andrew asked.

"That's how it works—the compounding part," said Mr. Sharp. "I find it easiest to think about like this: Compound interest is interest earned on interest. You see, interest is the money your money earns in an investment account. It's like free money. Just by sitting in the account, it earns money. Then the money that appeared for free begins to earn interest and generate its own free money. It has a 'compounding' effect—the interest earns interest."

"It's cool and all but it's not like it's that much money," Andrew said. "The interest on one hundred dollars is, what, a few dollars? So, the interest earned on that few dollars will be only a few pennies. I get the concept and all, but I wouldn't say it is the best thing in the world."

"Then you'd be disagreeing with none other than Albert Einstein. He once said that compound interest was the eighth wonder of the world. In fact, here's the quote attributed to him:

'He who understands it, earns it; he who doesn't, pays it.'"

"Sounds like it's better to understand it," said Andrew.

"You see," said Mr. Sharp, "compound interest is amazing because it seems, like you said, to be so little at first. A few pennies on the dollar. But the secret ingredient to compound interest is time. It lurks in the shadows, seeming to not exist, for quite some time and then suddenly it comes rushing in and your money exponentially increases. Have you heard of a hockey stick graph?"

Andrew looked at him blankly.

"OK, well you've heard of a hockey stick, right?"

"Sure."

"A hockey stick graph is just that—picture a hockey stick lying on its side with the tip facing up. For a long time, the graph is flat and flat and flat and then *BOOM*"—Mr. Sharp hit the table suddenly, jarring Andrew—"it shoots up. Like this …" He raced to the whiteboard in a rush of enthusiasm and drew a straight line horizontally across most of the board and then he shifted and drew the line at a much sharper angle.

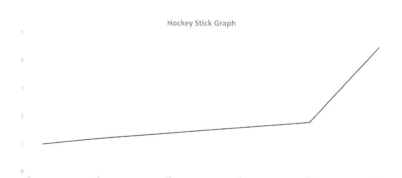

Hockey Stick Graph

"That," he said, "is the power of compound interest. Check it out …" Mr. Sharp pulled up a blank web page on his computer and typed in "compound interest calculator." "If we put in $1,800 for our initial investment and $200 for our monthly contribution and 10 percent for our rate of return, watch what happens when we put in thirty-nine for the number of years." Mr. Sharp hit the "calculate" button.

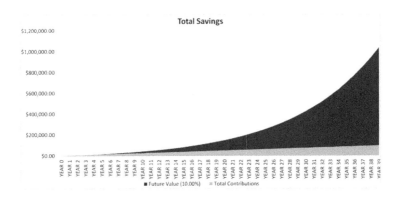

"Wow, $1,037,535.27," said Andrew, staring at the screen.

"Wow is right. Compound interest. You see at the beginning, you barely notice it because, you're right, it's just the interest on the interest you are earning. You're making $180 in interest the first year, so 10 percent of that is just $18. But compounded, year after year, and it adds up like crazy. Here, look at this …" Mr. Sharp pointed at the bottom line on the graph. "See here? This is how much money you contributed over those thirty-four years. $95,400. Just $95,400 of your own money—the other

$942,135 is interest. Compound interest. Mind-blowing, right?"

"Wait, is this for serious right now? Like $95,000 turned into a million dollars?"

"All serious. Completely. 100 percent. I remember when someone first showed this to me, I was in disbelief. I remember that night was the first night I started investing money. And I'm living proof that it works."

"What happens if I put more in? Like in a few years when I have a salary and all, what happens if I save like $500 a month?"

"Aha, I see you are catching the drift—trust me, this is probably the most fun you'll ever have with a calculator. Let's see—if you follow the plan for ten years, until you turn twenty-five, and then you up it to $500 …" Mr. Sharp began putting in the numbers into the computer. "You'd shave three years off."

"Three years? That's all? For more than doubling the contribution? That doesn't make any sense."

"That's the beauty and the problem with compound interest, Andrew. All the work is happening behind the scenes in the first ten to fifteen years. You see, let's say you started an investment plan when you were thirty-five years old, hoping to catch up to someone who started when they were fifteen. You have a good job, decent salary, and you save $500 a month. You would still get to a million dollars, but you'd be sixty-two years old when you did it, which is a far cry from being forty-nine. It's all about starting as early as possible. And starting at your age, well, you'd have a jump start on everyone else because I guarantee you they are not thinking about compound interest and investing."

"No," Andrew said, thinking of Kevin and smiling, "no, they are most definitely not. So what would happen if I just invested the $1,800 but didn't contribute any more to it? Do I still get compound interest?"

"You do indeed. In fact, here's a fun little bonus lesson for you—the rule of seventy-two. It looks something like this: Dividing the number seventy-two by your expected rate of return equals the number of years it would take to double your money. For instance, let's say you have an account that earns 6 percent interest a year. Seventy-two divided by six is twelve, so in twelve years, you would double your money. If you start with $1,800, it would be $3,600 in twelve years."

"Without me adding anything else to it?"

"Nothing else, just compound interest, your money earning money. A smart woman once told me, 'Your money works harder than you do.' And she was right—it works a lot harder, and it never stops working. Until you spend it, that is."

"What if I make 10 percent?"

"Hmm?" asked Mr. Sharp

"In the rule of seventy-two, if I make 10 percent, my money will double in just over seven years, right?"

"Yes, that is right, nicely done."

"So," Andrew said, scribbling as fast as he was talking, "that means that my $1,800 would double in seven years, and that $3,600 would double in seven more years, and …" Andrew stopped talking while he ran his fingers over his calculator. "That means that thirty-five years later, that $1,800 would be over $50,000. That's $48,200 in interest. Just from my money sitting there. That's crazy!"

"I told you your money worked hard. Between compound interest and the rule of seventy-two, it's clear that money makes money, which makes money. The only other ingredient is time. This is where shows like *Who Wants to Be a Millionaire*, as entertaining as they are, also drive me crazy. They portray this false reality of getting rich quick or accomplishing in one night what takes over thirty years to accomplish. Real millionaires do it the right way, slowly and steadily year after year until—"

"*BOOM!*" interjected Andrew, laughing.

"Yes, *BOOM*," said Mr. Sharp. "Incidentally, compound interest doesn't just apply to money. The concept is something you can apply to all sorts of areas in life in addition to the financial. Think about your ride to school, for example. How long does it take your parents to take you to school?"

"I don't know, maybe twenty-five minutes?"

"OK, and what do you listen to on the way in?"

"Music. We take turns. My mom gets Mondays and Thursdays, my dad gets Tuesdays, and I get Wednesdays and

Fridays. My dad only gets one day because he always chooses some rock band from the '80s that no one has ever heard of."

"Well, I salute him once again," said Mr. Sharp. "But think about it like this: 25 minutes twice a day is 50 minutes a day, which is 250 minutes a week. There are about thirty-six weeks in the school year, so that is 9,000 minutes or 150 hours. The average audiobook is between 6 and 10 hours in length, which means you could listen to about eighteen audiobooks a year. Now if you did that, for each year of high school, you would listen to seventy-two audiobooks just from your drive to and from school each day."

"Seventy-two books? That's more than I've read in my life!"

"And more than most people ever read in their lives. But consider if you did that, starting now, and established a habit, you'd have the chance to read, or rather listen to, over one thousand books in the span of a lifetime. And even if only a portion of those books were financial books, or self-improvement books, think about the cumulative wisdom you would gain."

"Well, I don't know about cumulative wisdom, but that is sure a lot of books."

"That's just one example. Think about how compound interest could apply to sports, or theater, or any other pursuit. Even your job at The Twist. Speaking of your job, I should probably get you out of here so you're not late. Assignment for this week: Come up with ways you can apply compound interest to other areas of your life. Get creative."

"Thanks, Mr. Sharp," Andrew said, getting up to leave. "This was pretty cool stuff."

"Thank *you*, Andrew," said Mr. Sharp. "And I agree, it is pretty cool."

That night, around the dinner table, Andrew regaled his parents with fact after fact about compound interest and how he could be a millionaire before he turned fifty.

"I have to say," Andrew's father said, leaning back in his chair, "I wish I had taken this class about thirty years ago."

"You're not the only one who wishes you had taken this class thirty years ago, honey," Andrew's mother said, giving his father a smile. "But the past is the past, and at least Andrew is learning these things before he learns them the hard way."

"So, are you going to do it?" his father asked.

"Do what?"

"Go for it—become a millionaire by age fifty?"

"Actually," Andrew said, smiling, "I ran some numbers and, well, I have a slightly different goal. Let's just say, I might be retiring early."

"That's the spirit," Andrew's dad said. "Perhaps we should pop open that pint of ice cream to celebrate."

CHAPTER SIX
SETTING GOALS

"Well, Andrew, what did you come up with?" Mr. Sharp asked when Andrew showed up in room 205 for the next class.

"For my assignment?"

"Yes," said Mr. Sharp. "You were supposed to think of ways to apply the concepts behind compound interest to other areas of your life."

"I had a conversation with my parents about everything we discussed, and they had all kinds of ideas. A few too many, actually," Andrew said, smiling.

"Ah, parents," said Mr. Sharp.

"My dad kept saying how much he wished he knew about compound interest early in life. He said that compound interest favors the young."

"Indeed it does," said Mr. Sharp. "The earlier you master the concept of compound interest, the more rewards it will reap in your life."

"Well, I thought about how I could apply it to other areas and I came up with four ideas. My parents said to organize it like this."

Andrew pulled a chart from his folder and handed it to Mr. Sharp. The chart had a line drawn down the middle vertically and a line down the middle horizontally to create four sections.

"Wow," said Mr. Sharp, "I love this. Your parents don't happen to be fans of Stephen Covey, do they?"

"I have no idea who that is," Andrew said.

"He wrote a famous book called *The 7 Habits of Highly Effective People* and in it, he suggests designing your weekly calendar or to-do list using the same format. In the top left quadrant, you put 'urgent' and 'important' items, in the top right one you put 'not urgent' and 'important' items, bottom left you put 'urgent' and 'not important' items, and in the final quadrant in the bottom right corner you put 'not urgent' and 'not important' items."

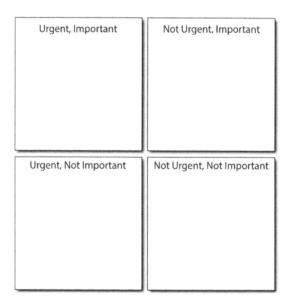

Mr. Sharp drew a sample on the whiteboard and labeled each section.

"According to Covey, most people get bogged down in the top left quadrant, the 'urgent' and 'important' one." Mr. Sharp gestured to the chart. "This is the problem—if we get bogged down there with the stuff that has to be done and be done quickly, we don't save the time necessary to work in the most important quadrant." Mr. Sharp pointed to the top right quadrant—the 'not urgent' and 'important' one.

"This quadrant," Mr. Sharp continued, "is where the really important things are found. Let's say you really want to write a screenplay for a movie, or start an online business, but you never have time to start because you are always working on homework or going to practice—"

"Or working at my job that someone told me to get," Andrew said with a smirk.

"Yes, or 'working at your job.' These are all important things that are also urgent. But the point is that if we make time and prioritize the things in this second quadrant, we will experience true success. Not only that, but we will find more freedom in our schedules. I don't even know how you high schoolers do it—balancing all the classwork with everything else. But I got ahead of myself, as usual. Tell me, what were the four sections on your chart about?"

"Well, I thought about what you said about compound interest and how I can apply it to other areas of my life. I thought the audiobook thing was cool and it inspired me to think of ways that I can really work to improve with small steps. I decided that I would focus on four areas: school, friends, work, and sports."

"I see a noticeable lack of 'family,'" Mr. Sharp said in a teasing manner.

"Yeah, I thought about that, but I figured that I had dinner with my parents almost every night anyway, so I didn't really need to work on that area too much. I mean family is, like, a given, right?"

"You'd be surprised, Andrew. As you get older, you realize more and more how important it is to invest your most important asset into your family. Do you remember your most important asset?"

"Time."

"That's right. We only have a set amount and can't get more. Let's talk about the categories you specified. What are your thoughts on school?"

"I usually get pretty good grades, mostly B's, but I got to thinking that if I invested a little more time in certain key areas, I could probably get some A's this quarter. Then I figured if I started getting A's, I'd become an A student, and probably get some scholarships or something."

"I love it. We'll return to this more in our discussion today but tell me about your 'friends' block."

"My best friend, Kevin, and I have been friends since kindergarten, and we always hang out. At least until recently. Once I got the job and everything, it's been harder to find the time. But at the same time, I don't really just want to sit around and watch shows, which is pretty much all we do. And I even started thinking that I should maybe start to get some new friends too. I don't know, but I mean I thought if I started working a little bit each week on making new friends, I'd probably have a few by the end of the year."

"Andrew, you seem to have really put some thought into this assignment and that pleases me," said Mr. Sharp. "I don't want to turn this into a therapy session—you can head over to the guidance office for that—but I am intrigued by your keen observations regarding friends. If I had one chief regret from high school and college, it would be not branching out more and making more friends. Starting the process of making friends, especially in new and different friend groups, is something that will alter the course of your life for the better."

"Yeah, well, so, anyway, the third area was work."

"Ah yes, tell me about your plans for The Twist."

"I thought about it, and I decided that if I start looking for ways to apply myself and stand out, I might get a raise, and if I get a raise, I can put a little more money into an investment account and start earning that compound interest even quicker. I asked a few of my coworkers and apparently they do raises every quarter and it is usually twenty-five or fifty cents an hour. Once in a while, though, someone gets a dollar raise. I thought if I really worked at it, I might earn one of those."

"And I see no reason why you wouldn't. How about the last category, sports?"

"I run cross country in the fall—we are midway through our season right now—and I do the two-mile track in the spring. Both are running sports, so I thought if I started doing a daily sprinting routine, I could really shave some time off my personal record."

"I ran cross country back when I was in high school—what's your current personal record?"

"I ran a 21:07 at the last meet, and that was by far my best."

"Not bad, not bad. You hoping to break 20:00 in the near future?"

"By the end of the season, hopefully."

"Well this is all the perfect transition into today's discussion and honestly, I feel like you have already done all of the work on this topic already. We're going to discuss setting goals and why that is key to your financial future. And the rest of your life too, for that matter. Andrew, the fact of the matter is that a person will only be as successful as the goals that person sets. Without goals, we accomplish little to nothing. But simply setting goals is not enough—we have to work to set goals that challenge us while not crushing us. For instance, if you set the goal to be a millionaire by the time you graduated high school, well, that goal would either crush you or you would have to give up on it altogether."

"Unless I landed a spot on the TV show."

"OK, so that's true I suppose. Another example would be if you said you were going to PR at 14:00 by the end of the season. Not only is that near impossible, but it would only discourage you once you realize you'll not make it. A goal has to be attainable but also has to represent a vital challenge in order to fully attain it. I simply can't stress this enough—without a goal, there can be no forward progress. And it is important that goals be set in each area of life—much like you did with the chart you just showed me. That chart, if you adhere to it, will improve your life in more ways than you can possibly imagine. Here, let me show you something." Mr. Sharp reached into his faded leather bag and pulled out a well-worn book and laid it on the table.

"*The Magic of Thinking Big,*" Andrew said. "I think I've heard of that book somewhere."

"It's almost as famous as *The 7 Habits of Highly Effective People*. It's also one of my favorite books. I keep a copy in my bag at all times and, as you can see"—Mr. Sharp held the book up to show Andrew its tattered condition—"it has been well-loved."

"You're not going to ask me to read that, are you? Because between cross country and work and my other assignments, I don't really have time for reading a book right now."

"No, I'm not going to ask you to read it. But I am going to ask you to listen to it. In fact, I have a feeling that your parents will be perfectly fine with playing an audiobook for the next few weeks or so while you drive to and from school.

They might even get a thing or two out of the book. But for now, I'm going to give you three primary points that pertain to the 'thinking big' concept that the book is all about."

Mr. Sharp went to the whiteboard and wrote, in big letters, "Principle One."

"First," he said, turning to Andrew, "is be the kind of person who exudes confidence. Not just 'be confident' but go a step further—be the kind of person who comes across as confident, who acts in a confident manner. For instance, do you have assigned seats in all your classes?"

"Most but not in English."

"And where do you sit in English?" asked Mr. Sharp.

"Kind of in the middle. Not the back or anything; I know not to do that."

"Well, I want you to do one better—I want you to sit in the front. The very front. I want you to be the kind of person who sits in the front of class and who takes notes, even if you're never going to look at the notes again. The person who does that is someone who says, 'I'm taking this seriously and I'm taking myself seriously.' And the type of person who exudes that display of confidence ends up going places."

"Not to be rude or anything, but what does this have to do with money and finance?"

"It may seem unrelated, but it is more related than meets the eye. The people who go around exuding confidence are the people who get the job, who get the promotion, who get the raise. They are the people who rise to the top, who dream bigger than everyone else, who experience the sweetness of success. Think about the last time you had a class discussion in your English class. Who spoke first? Who controlled the discussion? Does that person always speak first? How often do you speak? A confident person speaks first and speaks often."

"I thought it was more important to listen than to speak. At least that's what teachers are always saying."

"And I agree with that. In fact, one of the seven habits in Stephen Covey's book is all about listening first to understand before speaking to be understood. But my point is that while you don't have to be annoying about it, you do have to speak up and be heard to be noticed, and confident people are noticed. Wallflowers are not noticed. There's nothing necessarily wrong with just fading into the background, but if you get into a habit of doing that, you become content with just existing on the margins of life. Confident people speak up and are heard. They know they have worth and they embrace it."

Mr. Sharp paused to let Andrew catch up in his note-taking. Although most of Andrew's writing was illegible, Mr. Sharp was pleased to see that Andrew's notebook was almost half full by this point.

"Are you ready for Principle Two?" asked Mr. Sharp.

"Ready," said Andrew.

"Here goes—'act now.'"

Andrew wrote the words and circled them in his notes.

Mr. Sharp waited for him to look up and then said, "You go ahead and explain that one to me. What does it mean?"

"'Act now' means to not wait but go ahead and do it. Like Nike—Just Do It."

"Yes, like Nike. The world is full of sitters and doers. Sitters just sit. They do nothing. They may have an idea or an original thought from time to time, but they do nothing about it and so the idea dies. Doers take action. The author of the book, David Schwartz, says 'action cures fear.' What's something you hate doing?"

Andrew paused and looked up, caught off guard.

"Seriously," said Mr. Sharp. "Think of something that you just don't like doing and you always put it off as long as possible."

"Trash," said Andrew. "Taking out the trash. Every Thursday night I have to do it and I hate it because I have to break down all the boxes in the garage and everything from the week is piled up and I have to sift through it. It takes forever."

"Consider this," said Mr. Sharp. "What if, instead of waiting until Thursday night to break down all the boxes and sift through everything, what if you did it every time a new box went to the garage? What if you took action and broke the boxes down throughout the week? Then when Thursday rolled around, you wouldn't have to dread doing the trash because you already took care of the worst part."

"Makes sense," said Andrew. "But easier said than done."

"Exactly—if it was easy, everyone would do it. But the

payoff of taking action is huge. Just about everyone has one or two amazing ideas for a new business or invention or book or something throughout their lives. But few people ever act on these ideas and often those who do, give up before the thing is accomplished.

"Don't be one of those people—write your ideas down, review them, and then act on them. Take your chart, for example," said Mr. Sharp, holding up Andrew's compound interest assignment. "This is a great example of some amazing ideas, some key goals. But if you don't act on these, then nothing will be accomplished and the whole assignment will have been a waste of time. You have to take action to get things done. And before you ask about how this relates to finance—"

"I can see how," Andrew said, interrupting. "If you sit around and dream about earning money, you won't actually get up and go earn it."

"Precisely," said Mr. Sharp, giving Andrew a fist bump. "Precisely."

"So, what's the third?" asked Andrew.

"The third what?" asked Mr. Sharp.

"The third principle? You said you were going to talk about three principles from the book. What's the last one?"

"Geez, you rushing me, or what?" asked Mr. Sharp, smiling. "OK, here it is—'set goals for growth.'"

"'Set goals for growth'? Isn't that what we've been talking about this whole time?"

"It is, but consider that here we are talking about actually writing the goals down and establishing a plan to complete them. Look at the goals you wrote down on your chart. You want to work hard at your job so you can get a raise. That's a solid goal—and a fairly short-term one. I want you to start mapping out goals as soon as one month and as long as ten years. Take the main areas you want to establish goals in, like the areas you mapped out on your chart, and ask yourself, 'Where do I want to be in ten years with this area? How do I get there?' Then break it down into smaller goals for three years, and one year, and a few months."

"Ten years—I'll be twenty-five," said Andrew.

"Yes, but it is never too early to start planning ahead for that. If you know where you *want* to be at age twenty-five, you've got a much better chance of getting there than if you never thought about it. Goals are necessary for success, but they have to be specifically worded or they just become some blanket statement. Most goals can be improved if they are planned using the '*S-M-A-R-T*' acronym. Have you heard that one before?"

Andrew shook his head.

"OK, here goes," Mr. Sharp said, turning to the whiteboard. He wrote SMART in large letters aligned vertically on the board, and then he started filling in each letter going across. "*S* is for specific, *M* is for measurable, *A* is for achievable, *R* is for relevant, and *T* is for time-based. Each goal you set should have a specific, measurable, achievable, relevant, and time-based component."

"Here's what I mean," continued Mr. Sharp. "You want to get a one-dollar raise, right?"

"Right," said Andrew.

"That's great, you see, you already did the S—it's a specific goal. A one-dollar raise. As for measurable, you can determine how you are making progress by checking in with your manager from time to time to see if there is anything that can be improved. Be honest and say, 'I want to really succeed at this job and prove myself worthy of a raise. Can you tell me how I can improve my performance, so I bring more value to the company?'"

"I'm not sure how long you've been out of school, Mr. Sharp, but around here, we call that kind of person a 'brown-noser' or a 'suck-up.'"

"That's weird, because when I was in school, we called that person a 'kiss-ass.'"

Both Andrew and Mr. Sharp laughed at this for several moments.

"But seriously, Andrew," said Mr. Sharp, "I totally get the

fear of coming across as someone just trying to suck up, but remember what cures fear?"

"Action," Andrew said, looking back at an underlined section in his notes. "Action cures fear."

"Exactly, and you have to be the kind of person who sees what he wants and goes after it. If you really want that one-dollar raise, you must make it clear to your superiors that you are working to improve, and you'll put in whatever extra effort necessary. That brings us to A, attainable. Do you reasonably believe a one-dollar raise is possible?"

"I know it has happened before, but I know it is pretty rare. Only a few people have ever gotten it."

"Sounds like it is challenging but doable, so it definitely qualifies. As for R, relevant, I think you have that nailed. You mentioned you wanted a raise so you could invest even more money, and that seems to align with the overall goal of attaining wealth, so you're on track there. Now let's talk T, time-based. The final step to a goal is giving yourself a specific time to complete the goal. You mentioned that raises were determined quarterly—any idea when the next time is?"

"Well, I got hired at the start of September, and I think the last round of evaluations was right after that, so I guess probably the start of December?"

"Let's set a specific date—how about December 15? That's the end of the semester, and this class, so it's an easy one to remember. By December 15, you will have a one-dollar raise. Notice my wording there ..." Mr. Sharp wrote on the whiteboard "will" and circled it. "I didn't say 'might' or 'hope to' but 'will.' Leave no room for chance or half-hearted commitments. A goal has to be such that you can fully give in to it and work to bring it about knowing that it will come about."

Andrew stopped writing and stared down at his notes. After a moment or two of silence, he spoke up.

"Mr. Sharp, here's my question: If I create a goal, say to earn a one-dollar raise, then I'm going to have to dedicate a lot of time and effort to reaching that goal. I'll probably have to stay later at work or go in earlier or think of ways to improve that will take up time from other areas. So how am I supposed to set goals in other areas, like my running or my grades, if I'm committing everything to the one goal? Does that make sense? Like you keep saying, 'time is my most precious resource,' but how can I dedicate enough to all of these areas and all of these goals?"

"Andrew, that is perhaps the chief problem at the center of goal making," said Mr. Sharp. "And it comes down to one word: prioritize. This is where you must decide how to take charge of your life. Just like the person who acts with confidence, you must decide what your priorities in life are going to be. Are you going to be someone who prioritizes his goals, or someone whose life gets so busy that he forgets about his goals and then never accomplishes them? Think back to that chart I shared with you that labels things based on whether it is 'urgent' and 'important.'

"You have to look at all the areas of your life and make some decisions. You must decide which things will get your full attention and which things you will let slip. The fact of the matter is that the sooner you realize you cannot do everything, the better. So often we try to convince people, and high schoolers in particular, that they have to be involved in everything. They have to participate in sports, be in school plays, participate in orchestra, be part of the honors society, lead a service group, be active in their church, and still find time to be with their family and their friends."

"Dang, sounds like you know a thing or two about being in high school," said Andrew.

"Let's just say I saw the experience drag my daughter down considerably. Fortunately, I had worked with her since a young age to help her prioritize; otherwise, I'm afraid she would have encountered much stress. Some of her friends were not so fortunate. Look, Andrew, I can't stand here and tell you what you should value above other things in your life. But the thing about goals is that if you commit to them, you'll have to, by necessity, drop other things in your life. Life is, ultimately, about choices, and when we choose to go after something, we must focus on that thing and not get distracted by the many things that try to grab our attention.

"I once heard a great illustration for this—imagine that you are juggling and you keep adding more and more balls to what you are juggling. Soon you have about eight balls in the air and some of them are made of glass while some are made of rubber. If you drop a rubber one, it bounces, and all is fine. But if you drop a glass one, it shatters and is gone. We must determine which of the balls we are juggling are made of glass and which of rubber—which ones we can let fall and be fine, and which ones we need to make sure stay in the air."

"Prioritize the glass balls," said Andrew. "Basically, figure out which things have to be done, or are essential, and let other things fall."

"Exactly," said Mr. Sharp. "The stage of life you are in right now is all about introducing you to new ideas, concepts, and opportunities. But sometimes, this comes with the risk of taking on too much at once, too many balls in the air. So many things try to grab our attention and pull us in multiple directions at once. You must be strong and tell yourself that you are goal-driven and focused and will not be distracted. And it's hard—it's hard as a high schooler, and it's hard as an adult. I'm not sure it ever gets easier, but one thing that helps, for sure, is seeing the accomplishments pile up from the dedication to goals."

"Where do I start?" Andrew asked.

"Start with big-term life goals. Forget ten years. Ask yourself what you want most out of life. Look at it from all the major categories—family, career, finances, accomplishments, and so on. Then work backward to see where you have to be in ten years to meet those goals, in five years, in three years, in one year, and so on. That way, you begin working toward those long-term life goals with each decision you make on a daily basis. If you have the life goal of writing a book, then start writing a few pages each day to get in the habit. If you want to become a professional athlete, then start a practice regime that you keep every day."

"Like compound interest again," Andrew said.

"It all comes back to compound interest. Compound interest is what drives goal attainment. These big, looming goals can never be accomplished with one or two little steps. But, like the seed tree, one or two little steps every day for year and year after year compounds and then—"

"*BOOM*," Andrew said, beating Mr. Sharp to the punch.

"Ha! Yes, *BOOM*—the hockey stick."

"Um, Mr. Sharp," Andrew said, pointing to the clock on the wall.

"Good grief," said Mr. Sharp, "how the time flies when you are waxing eloquently. Well, you've got your assignment—listen to the audiobook version of *The Magic of Thinking Big*. And while you're doing that, come up with some clear goals that align with the SMART acronym."

"Sounds good," Andrew said, getting up to leave. He made his way out of the door and headed down the hall when he realized he had forgotten his notebook. He had just turned around to head back to the room when Mr. Sharp exited, notebook in hand.

"Missing something?" Mr. Sharp teased, smiling. "I'm headed to the parking lot, so I'll walk with you for a bit."

"Hey, Mr. Sharp," Andrew asked as they headed to the stairwell, "we talked a lot about my goals and everything. What are your goals? Any interesting ones you're working on?"

"It's funny; I usually don't get that question. There is one in particular that I'm focused on right now," said Mr. Sharp. "I've always wanted to write a book."

"I thought maybe you'd say that since you kept mentioning it. Are you wanting to write a fiction book?"

"Well, yes and no," said Mr. Sharp. "Actually, I've been thinking that I might write a book about finance and why high school students should start now to learn all about managing money. Sort of the principles I talk about in class with you."

"And have you started writing it?"

"Technically no," said Mr. Sharp, "not yet. But I—"

"Aha!" Andrew said, smiling. "Sounds like someone has some homework to do. Sounds like you need to sit down and develop a SMART plan for that goal."

"You know what," Mr. Sharp said, patting Andrew on the back, "You're right. I can't ask you to do something I'm not working on myself. Sounds like we both have some goals to sketch out for our next class."

CHAPTER SEVEN
THE WHY

Later that day, as Andrew was putting on his shirt featuring a giant soft pretzel with "The Twist" in gold cursive writing, he thought back over his conversation with Mr. Sharp. If he really wanted to pursue the goal of getting a raise, maybe he should bring up the subject with a shift manager to see what he had to say. After all, Mr. Sharp seemed to think it couldn't hurt.

That evening, during a lull in customers, Andrew saw that Steve was staring intently at a clipboard. Steve was the shift manager on weeknights—he was about nineteen years old and was a freshman at an online college. Steve was nice enough and never gave Andrew any trouble, so Andrew summoned up his courage and walked over.

"Hey, Steve, do you have a sec?" he asked.

"Yeah, sure, what do you need?"

"Well, I was just thinking, I mean, I heard that once a quarter everyone gets reviewed, and some people get raises."

"Ah, and let me guess, you're wondering how you can get a raise?"

"Yes, I mean, well, I just wanted to know what I could do to improve and bring value to the company."

"'Bring value to the company?' What are you, a junior executive? This is a soft pretzel business in a mall, man; none of us actually wants to be here. Look, dude, I'm going to shoot you straight cos I like you. Just do your job, don't cause trouble, and you'll probably get twenty-five cents more per hour in a few months. I mean, I'm a manager and I've been here over a year and I'm only getting seventy-five cents more an hour than when I started. Best I can say is just do your thing and get paid."

"OK, sounds good. Thanks," Andrew said as he headed back to the register. "That did not go as planned," he thought to himself. "So much for that."

Somewhat disheartened by the experience, Andrew put a lackluster effort into his assignment for Mr. Sharp and, when the next class rolled around, handed the paper in with almost no enthusiasm.

"Thanks, Andrew," said Mr. Sharp. "Tell me about these goals."

"They're pretty much the same ones we talked about last class. I want to get a raise at work, I want to run a 19:30 race, and I want to get all A's."

"What about the big life goals?" Mr. Sharp asked. "And how about the SMART aspect? This one about getting a raise, for example. I don't see the amount on here. Is there a reason you aren't being specific?"

"I don't know," Andrew said in a dejected tone. "Not much hope in anything more than the twenty-five-cent raise everyone else gets."

"That's a decidedly different outlook than you had in the last class. Did something happen?"

Andrew filled Mr. Sharp in on his conversation with the shift manager and how he was told to just do his thing and keep his head down.

"I see," said Mr. Sharp after a short pause. "And, Andrew, just who was this manager of yours you talked to?"

"Steve—he's a nice guy; he tells it like it is."

"Can you describe Steve as a worker?"

"He's younger so we all like him more than some of the other managers. He's also cool and doesn't care if we use our phones if there are no customers. Overall, he's pretty laid-back and casual, I guess."

"Who are some of the other managers at The Twist?"

"Well, only two that I've worked with—Carol and Dan. Carol is older and doesn't really like us to mess around. She always gives Steve a certain look when he is being goofy. Steve does a hilarious impression of her when she's not around."

"And what about Dan?"

"Dan is Dan. Like he's quiet and just does his stuff and doesn't really talk much."

"It sounds like Carol sort of runs the show and follows the rules; is that accurate?" asked Mr. Sharp.

"Yeah, I guess. I mean, she's always making sure we're doing our job and our shirts are tucked in and we're not on our phones. She says there's always something to do—we could be cleaning or restocking or organizing. Whenever she's on the shift, it's bound to be a long night."

"Have you ever met the owners of The Twist? Do you know who they are?"

"No, they've never come around. As far as I know, Carol is in charge, but all three of them oversee the store."

"Andrew, I obviously don't work there and don't want to presume too much, but just based on what you've shared with me, I think I have a fairly good handle on how things run at your store. Do you mind if I offer you some pointers?"

"Go ahead," said Andrew.

"First, let me ask this—what would you say is the main reason why The Twist is in business. What is the big 'Why' driving the store?"

"The big 'Why'?" asked Andrew.

"I'm borrowing it from a writer named Simon Sinek. He has an inspiring TED talk called 'Start with Why' that turned into a book that—"

"That, let me guess, you think I should read?" Andrew asked.

"You're probably thinking that all I do is recommend books you should read. There's just so much great material out there that I don't want you to miss any of it. I mean, next to time, your mind is your greatest asset and investing in its growth is always worthwhile. Are you familiar with a cost-benefit analysis?"

"We did those last year for a debate unit. You make a chart and look at the costs of something and compare it to the benefits to see which is better."

"Apply that to a book like the ones I've mentioned. These books cost something like twelve or fifteen dollars."

"Like an hour and a half at The Twist," Andrew said.

"Exactly," said Mr. Sharp. "These books cost you an hour and a half of your time in money and then a few hours of your time in reading. So the cost is something like five or six hours, depending on the book. But the benefit can be enormous—if it teaches you something, even just one thing, that you can apply to your life to improve your situation, then it is worth far more than six hours."

"Especially if I get them from the library and don't even buy them," said Andrew.

"Sometimes I think you should be teaching the class," Mr. Sharp said with a smile. "Let's go back to the question at hand. What would you say is the big Why driving The Twist."

"I don't know, to make money, I guess?"

"Sure, most businesses strive to make money and without making money, a business cannot stay in business. But making money is not a Why—a Why is something larger, something that drives the business to higher levels. A Why is what gets customers excited and creates raving fans. Let's try a different question: Where is The Twist located?"

"Well, it's in a mall."

"Where in the mall?"

"On the main floor, the bottom floor, across from American Eagle and Gap."

"And what does The Twist sell?"

"Soft pretzels. All different ones—cinnamon sugar, butter, jalapeno. Also drinks."

"So, The Twist is a food establishment inside the mall. Why is it not in the food court?" asked Mr. Sharp.

"Well, it doesn't sell 'food' exactly—more like snacks or a treat. Like something you want to pick up while you're shopping but don't necessarily want to sit down to eat."

"Is it fair to say that The Twist offers customers a chance to enhance the mall experience by providing a culinary diversion?"

"I don't know about 'culinary' but I guess it provides people with something tasty while they're walking around."

"Would you say it makes their day a little bit better when they come by?"

"I guess—we're supposed to say 'Make it an awesome day' when a customer leaves. No one actually does, well, unless Carol is around, but it's so cheesy that we don't like saying it."

"Last question—when a customer comes to The Twist, who do they interact with primarily?"

"Me, or, well, whoever is working the register."

"So whoever is working the register is the person who interacts directly with the customer."

Andrew nodded.

"And making customers happy is what keeps The Twist in business?"

Andrew nodded again.

"Just to clarify—what you're telling me is that, because you work the register, you are the person responsible for keeping The Twist in business?"

"I never thought about it like that before," Andrew said, "but I guess that's right. I mean, if a customer gets upset, she might never come back."

"Do you suppose Steve and Dan and Carol all know why The Twist is in business?"

"Sure—they're the managers."

"And do you suppose they have a vested interest in the business doing well?"

"Yeah."

"It sounds to me, from your description, that the only one who really cares about how the business is doing is Carol. It sounds like she may be frustrated with her other managers and some of her employees because they don't care about the business in the same way she does. Do you suppose she knows that the only reason you all say 'Make it an awesome day' is because she's around?"

"Probably, I mean we usually whisper, 'Carol's on tonight' to warn everyone when they show up for their shift."

"And how do you think that makes her feel that she is the only one following the rules, and everyone dislikes her for it?"

Andrew was starting to catch on.

"All I'm suggesting, Andrew, is that if you are serious about your goals for your work, you need to consider how you present yourself in the business. If you are just going to do what it takes to get by, like Steve, then yes, you'll have to settle for a twenty-five cents an hour raise. But if you are going to go for it, and I mean *really* go for it, you're going to have to think a little differently about your approach."

Andrew was silent for a bit. Finally, he said, "Mr. Sharp—I didn't really put much effort into my goals this week. I kind of got discouraged after my conversation with Steve, and I just kind of turned in a weak attempt. Any chance I can redo the assignment?"

"Absolutely and thanks for your honesty, Andrew. Setting big goals for yourself is not something to take lightly, so why don't you take the rest of class to really brainstorm and think through how you want to approach these."

"Thanks, sounds good. I'll have something much better next time."

"I have no doubt, Andrew. And good luck with The Twist—be sure to keep me posted on how things turn out."

Later that evening, after helping to clear the dishes, Andrew sat back down at the table with his class notebook and a pen. At the top of the page at which he was now staring was written "Add Value" and underneath was the start of a list. Andrew continued staring at the partially finished list and finally dropped his pen and let out an exasperated groan.

"What's wrong, honey?" asked his mother, who was sitting at her computer in the next room. "Homework got you down?"

"No, well, kind of. It's this thing for Mr. Sharp. It's nothing; I'll figure it out."

"If it's coming from Mr. Sharp's class, then I'm sure it's not 'nothing,'" said his mother, getting up to walk into the kitchen. "I hear he's giving you lots of good ideas about your future."

"Well, we're talking about goals now and I told him I want to work to get a raise at The Twist. I'm supposed to think of ways I can 'add value' at work in order to accomplish the goal. Mr. Sharp says that if you make yourself valuable, the pay will follow. Or something like that."

"You do know," said his mother, sitting down at the table, "that this is the kind of thing that is up my alley."

"It is?" Andrew asked.

"Yes, it is—I conduct interviews throughout my company to determine promotions, raises, and demotions."

"I thought you worked in HR," Andrew said.

"I do, but there is a lot more to HR than just hiring. I like to think of my position as more about promotions and helping people determine their path, even if that is a path that leads outside the company. It's about what is best for the individual, as well as the company. So, tell me a little bit about what's going on at work," she said, settling into her "work mindset."

After Andrew had filled her in on everything from Mr. Sharp's class to his work at The Twist, she leaned back and stared past Andrew's head for a few moments. After what seemed like an eternity, she spoke.

"Well, honey, I can't just tell you what to do, even though I suspect that's what you want."

Andrew gave her a look of mock frustration.

"You didn't let me finish—I can't tell you what to do because you need to figure that out for yourself. But I can tell you what stands out in my company when it comes to adding value. The people who work to add value fall into two camps: those who just want a pay raise and those who sincerely want to make the company better. There's nothing wrong with those who just want a pay raise—in fact, they often add quite a bit of value to the company. But, in the end, they'll jump ship as soon as they get a better offer. No, the people who really, truly add value, the people I seek out for promotions and for positions with larger responsibility are the ones who understand the company's mission and use themselves, selflessly, to improve the entire environment."

"So, like, the martyrs?" Andrew asked.

"Nice word choice but no, not exactly martyrs. When I say 'selfless,' I mean someone who is not just out to make a name for themselves, but someone who cares more about what is best for the company. These are the people who, instead of self-promoting all the time, point out something awesome their coworker did. They help build morale and overall spirit. Those are the ones I seek out."

"But you're not just going to tell me what to do to be one of those people?"

"That's the thing, Andrew—I can't. If I told you, it would not be genuine. It's not something you can just turn on one day—it is something you must develop over time. But it is worth it, every step of the way. Either way, though, you'll always have your mother on your team," she said, smiling.

"Well thanks, but no thanks, Mom," Andrew said, smiling back. "I guess you just made my assignment more difficult."

"Glad I could help. Now if you want to help me, you could answer some of these emails sitting in my inbox."

"No thanks, I'll stick to this," Andrew said, gesturing toward his notebook. The rest of the evening was spent jotting down thoughts, crossing out ideas, and crumpling up sheets of paper. By the time Andrew was settling down for bed, his head was swimming with ideas, plans, and strategies. "Add value," he said out loud to no one in particular. "Selfless." With these thoughts, and more, Andrew drifted off to sleep.

His next shift at The Twist was after school on Thursday and as he got ready for his shift, he took a little extra time checking the mirror. He straightened his collar, tucked in his shirt, and brushed his hair to the side. Then he checked his teeth for any stray bits of food and gave himself a smile. "Make it an awesome day," he said, pointing at himself in the mirror. "Why thank you, and you, too," he said back, gesturing with both index fingers.

He felt incredibly goofy. But also ready.

His first customer was a clearly frazzled mother of three young children who ordered four pretzels—one cinnamon sugar, one regular with salt, one no salt, and one super lightly cooked with no browning and a very light dusting of salt. An order such as this would typically cause Andrew to inwardly (and sometimes outwardly) roll his eyes, but today, after handing the young mother her order, he made eye contact with her and said, with more enthusiasm than he thought he could muster, "Make it an AWESOME day!"

The mother looked back in alarm and replied, "Uh, thanks?" before heading off with her Tasmanian devil children, who were in various states of devouring soft pretzels.

"OK," Andrew thought to himself, "a bit much, but the right idea." He spent the next few hours fine-tuning his approach until he felt confident in his customer banter. A "What's up, welcome to The Twist home of the famous soft pretzel, what can I get for you?" was followed by a "Sure thing, coming right up," which was then, after the order was delivered, followed by a naturally enthusiastic "Make it an awesome day" and then, to Andrew's own surprise, a fist bump. The first customer he tried this on sort of looked at him and then returned the fist bump, but after that, the idea took off. By the end of his shift, customers were laughing and giving him enthusiastic fist bumps and a few even said, "You make it an awesome day, too," in response.

Andrew was exhausted by the time he got home and was asleep within minutes of hitting his pillow. The next few days flew by in a blur, and Andrew found himself with some free time due to Mr. Sharp being out of town and canceling class for the week. Andrew had started binge-watching a new series on Netflix but soon became distracted and began fiddling around with a new graphic design program. Before he knew it, he had designed a small, business-card size graphic containing the logo of The Twist interlaced with the words "Make It an Awesome Day." That night he printed several sheets of the graphic and cut them, painstakingly, by hand and took them to work that evening.

During his shift at The Twist, he embellished his "Make it an awesome day" and his fist bump by handing each customer one of his cards.

"Whatcha giving them?" Candace asked, poking her head over Andrew's shoulder after about his fifth customer. Candace, like Andrew, worked the front register on weeknights. She was a few years older than Andrew but had only been working at The Twist since the summer before.

"Just a little card I made," Andrew said.

"Can I see it?" Candace asked.

"Sure, it's just a little business card thing, nothing special," he said as he held up a card.

"Oh! My gosh! It's so cute!" Candace said, gushing over the card. "Can I keep one? Please?"

"I guess," Andrew said, blushing. Candace was an attractive girl whom Andrew had already noticed more than once while working his Thursday shifts.

"Thanks!" she said, returning to her work of buttering finished pretzels.

That evening, Andrew gave out over thirty cards, not to mention fist bumps and "Make it an awesome day" sayings. Strangely, at the end of his shift, he didn't feel exhausted as much as he felt elated—he felt like he could work another few hours without feeling drained. This feeling of elation, however, was not long-lasting. As soon as he showed up for his Saturday morning shift, his good vibes were about to take a turn.

"Hey, Andrew," Steve said, walking up as soon as Andrew had donned his work shirt. "Carol wants to see you in her office. Said it's urgent. Not sure what it's all about, but I can tell you nothing good comes from meeting Carol in her office. It was nice knowing you, dude!"

Andrew's heart fell from his chest and his feet, now filled with concrete, seemed unable to move. Carol wanted to see him? This could be nothing but bad. He considered his options: making a run for it, quitting on the spot, pretending to be sick. Nothing seemed to solve the problem. Then he remembered what Mr. Sharp had said about facing things head-on and getting the uncomfortable or frustrating things out of the way first. "Action cures fear," he said both to himself and out loud—a little too out loud.

"What's that?" Steve asked, looking up from his computer.

"Nothing," Andrew said from a quickly reddening face. He moved through the workstations and made his way to the back of the store toward the store manager's office. After a brief pause, he knocked.

"Come in," Carol's voice said from behind the door. Andrew slowly pushed the door open and walked inside.

"Ah, Andrew," Carol said in her typically blunt, forward manner, "I trust you are well?"

"Yes, yes ma'am, I am," Andrew said, wishing she would just jump to the part where he gets in trouble for something.

"Do you know why I asked to see you?" she asked.

"No, well, yes, I don't know," Andrew said.

"Can you explain this to me?" Carol asked, holding out a folded business card. Andrew took the card with trembling fingers and unfolded it. On the inside, next to a logo for The Twist were the words "Make It an Awesome Day!"

"This is, uh, well, it's just something I was giving out to customers. I'm sorry, I'll stop doing it. I just thought it might cheer them up." Andrew said, stammering to get the words out.

"You'll do nothing of the sort," Carol said with her characteristic lack of charm.

"Huh?" Andrew asked.

"You'll do nothing of the sort. Stop giving it out, I mean. I called you in here because I had a customer come up to me today asking if the 'boy who was handing out the cards' was working today. I asked her what she meant, and she pulled the card from her purse. She said you gave her the card a few days ago and that she kept the card with her since then and looked at it multiple times and it 'made her day.'"

Andrew stared in amazement.

"So, I called you back here to say good job and congratulate you. You really made a difference for that customer. Whatever gave you the idea to hand these cards out?"

"I don't know; I guess I just wanted to help out and add value," Andrew said.

"Add value?" Carol asked. "What do you mean 'add value'?"

"Well, I just wanted to go the extra step and, you know, make the customers feel valued. I mean without customers, we don't have a business, right? So, I wanted them to feel like they were important to us, like we cared. The cards were just an idea to express that."

"How old are you, Andrew?" Carol asked.

"I'm going to be sixteen in two weeks," Andrew replied.

"Andrew, I have people in their twenties and thirties working here who don't have as much initiative as you. You've really latched on to something with these cards. I don't want you to stop; in fact, I want you to keep going. Keep up the great work and just know that we appreciate what you are doing."

"Uh, thanks!" Andrew said as he got up to leave. He paused just before walking out of the office, took a deep breath, and turned around to face Carol.

"Can I ask you a question?" he said.

"Yes, what is it?"

"Is there anything I can do that would make your job easier?"

"Make my job easier?" she asked. "What do you mean?"

"It seems like you have a lot on your plate. I mean, you always seem really busy, and I was just wondering if I could help with anything."

"You really are a go-getter, aren't you? There is something—I have to get a count on all stock by the end of the day. In between customers, if you could help me get a count on everything in the front of the house, that would be a big help."

"I'm on it," Andrew said, smiling as he left the office.

With a renewed energy after his meeting with Carol, Andrew put everything he had into the rest of his shift. He was in the zone—from greeting customers to organizing stock, he was on fire and taking it to a new level. He was so focused, in fact, that he had to do a double-take when he realized the customer now standing at the register was none other than Kevin.

"What's up, dude?" Kevin asked. "I hear this is where I can snag some free pretzels."

"Hey, man," said Andrew. "What are you doing here? I didn't know you were coming tonight."

"It's your fault, really," said Kevin. "My parents are all like 'Andrew has a job, why can't you get a job?' and so I was finally like 'Fine, I'll go get a job!' and here I am."

"Wait, you want to work here?" Andrew asked, confused.

"Ha, no!" said Kevin. "I'd prefer to not have to wear a shirt that says 'The Twist' and greet everyone with 'Make it an awesome day!' Not for me. I'm applying at Gap. Just picked up an application and the dude working said as long as I was breathing, I was hired."

"That's cool," said Andrew. "We'll basically be working a few doors down from each other."

"Yeah," said Kevin, "at least this will give me some extra money—my parents said that if I want the new PlayStation, I have to pay for it. Anyway, I'm going to go fill this out. Later."

"Oh, Kevin," Andrew said as Kevin turned back.

"What?"

"Make it an awesome day!"

"Dude, you are such a nerd," Kevin said, smiling.

Andrew returned his focus to work and began to think about a system to help keep the stock organized. Before long, he had an idea and that evening, after he got home, he pulled up an Excel sheet and started designing a page. His class in computer applications had given him enough proficiency in Excel that he thought he could design a spreadsheet to track inventory in an easier manner. Before he knew it, it was 11 p.m. and time for him to head to bed. He saved the Excel sheet, turned off his computer, and got under the covers. Despite the creeping feeling of exhaustion, Andrew lay for several minutes staring up at his ceiling deep in thought. He thought about Carol and how she had said, "We appreciate what you are doing." He thought about Mr. Sharp and what he had said about setting goals. He thought about what his mother had said about adding value. Finally, with all these thoughts swimming in his head, he fell soundly asleep.

CHAPTER EIGHT
INTRODUCTION TO INVESTING

The next day, in room 205, Andrew brimmed over with excitement as he relayed the entire conservation to Mr. Sharp.

"Andrew, this is great news," Mr. Sharp said. "And living proof that daily work on big goals has a direct impact. It sounds like you are well on your way to achieving one of your primary goals, maybe even by Thanksgiving at this rate."

"I decided I wanted to focus more on adding value than just getting a raise. And it's been a blast—I genuinely enjoy going to work."

"I can tell," Mr. Sharp said. "This whole topic is actually the perfect transition into our topic for the next few classes: investing. We talked earlier when we were discussing compound interest that when you invest your money wisely, you get high returns that help your money generate more money. It's also true that if you invest your time and energy in a project, like you are at work, it can pay off with large returns in the end. But for all the wise investments out there, there are thousands of unwise ones. I'm going to focus today's class on long-term investing," Mr. Sharp said, drawing a hockey stick shape on the board. "Remember this graph?" he asked.

"Yes, compound interest—not much happens for a while, but then it shoots up."

"Exactly," said Mr. Sharp. "This is how long-term investing works. And the big component involved in long-term investing is time. Understanding the time value of money is a core fundamental of having financial intelligence. Time is where you have an advantage over almost everyone else in the investing world. While most people are looking at this in their late twenties or thirties, you are looking at it as a fifteen-year-old."

"Soon to be sixteen—my birthday is in less than two weeks."

"Happy pre-birthday," said Mr. Sharp. "Let's change our starting point to age sixteen, then. Consider that most people think of long term as in fifteen to twenty years. For you, however, long term can be almost double that or more. The typical retirement age is sixty-five and that's when most people try to plan the peak of their wealth-building so they can retire and live off the interest their money is earning. Most people also have nowhere near what they should in their retirement accounts and end up dependent on social security and other government benefits. The problem here is that those programs most likely will not be around when you retire, so you won't be able to depend on them. We must have a plan for you to have enough money saved up so that you can comfortably retire and not worry about money. With our ideal plan, you can retire early."

Andrew smiled.

"I know," said Mr. Sharp, "it's weird to be thinking about your retirement when you are about to turn sixteen, but it is so important to—"

"No, it's not that," Andrew said. "It's what you said about retiring early. I made that my long-term financial goal on my goal sheet. I want to retire early. Maybe not stop working, but at least stop feeling like I have to work."

"An excellent goal," said Mr. Sharp. "And one that is more than attainable when we think about long-term investing. And I like what you said about not feeling like you have to work. Often, we become so focused on retirement that we forget to enjoy what we are doing in the present. I'm not suggesting that you get so future-focused that you forgo having fun now, but if you are in a state of financial freedom, then you are not dependent on your income from your job and you are free to choose what you want to do.

"So financial freedom is about choice," Andrew said.

"Yes," said Mr. Sharp. "You have the choice regarding how to spend your time. Maybe you want to spend it on the golf course. Fine, go do it. Maybe you want to spend time with your children or even, dare I say, grandchildren. Fine, go do it. Maybe you want to donate time to work with a nonprofit or help in a school. Whatever it is, you are free to do it.

"Let's say that you plan on retiring at age fifty-five, a full ten years earlier than most people. That gives you about forty years to invest. Now, let's look at what that looks like in terms of numbers. If you save $186 a month—"

"Mr. Sharp," Andrew said, interrupting.

"Yes?"

"Can we make it $250 a month?"

"Well, that's certainly more than $186. I don't want you to set unrealistic goals early on. How would you go about meeting that goal?"

"If, I mean, *when* I meet my goals at work, I'll be able to increase my savings. I'm also not going to spend quite as much. I spent some time going over the budget we made, and I'm confident I can put $250 a month into long-term savings. I've actually decided to stop my Netflix subscription, and I'm going to cut a few other areas."

"OK then, let's plan on $250. Now, if you remember our calculations, we are looking at finding a way to earn 10 percent over the long term, and we are going to look at forty years. For the purposes of this plan, let's say that you are starting at $0."

Mr. Sharp plugged the numbers into his online interest calculator and pressed "calculate."

"Wow," said Andrew.

"I know," said Mr. Sharp. "Wow is right."

"Holy crap," said Andrew.

"That, too," said Mr. Sharp.

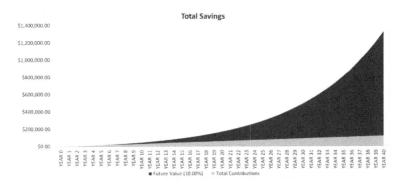

The calculator showed a red line that, after heading horizontally across the graph for the first twenty-four years, took a sharp turn up and became almost a vertical line. Where it ended, at year forty, the text read "Total Savings: $1,327,777.67."

"That's over $1 million!" Andrew said. "By age fifty-five. That's crazy!"

"And look at this," Mr. Sharp said as he plugged in a few more numbers. "If you keep going for ten more years and don't touch it until age sixty-five, the typical retirement age, here's what it would be."

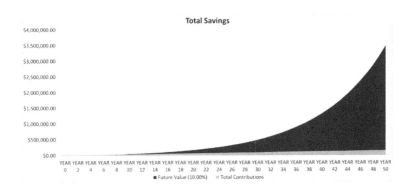

Andrew and Mr. Sharp stared at the screen for a few minutes without speaking. Finally, after a long period of silence, Andrew spoke.

"It's $3.4 million. That's a lot."

"Yes, it is," said Mr. Sharp.

"OK, slow down," said Andrew. "Is this for real? $3,491,725 by putting in $250 a month from age sixteen to age sixty-five?"

"Remember that we are assuming you are getting a 10 percent return on your investment. The number is considerably smaller if you are getting less than that. With 6 percent, you're going to see far, far less."

"Like half of that since it is half the return?" Andrew asked.

"You would think," said Mr. Sharp. "But then you'd be forgetting about how compound interest works. As the interest builds, that interest earns more interest. If you are making a 6 percent return year after year for all those years, then you would only get up to $871,000 by age sixty-five."

"Only $871,000? What? That's insane!"

"I know—that's why it is important to get the best rate of return possible. Every percentage point adds to your total amount exponentially. In a future class, I'll go into more depth on how to seek out those higher return investments."

"If getting to that kind of money really is that easy, then why don't more people do it? Does everyone retire with over $3 million?" asked Andrew.

"Not even close," said Mr. Sharp. "Two reasons: First, they don't know. Pure and simple, they just don't know. We don't teach it in schools, at least not normally—maybe you've realized by now that this is not a normal class. The school is not paying me to teach this class; I'm doing it on my own."

"You're doing all this for free?" asked Andrew.

"Yes, because I believe in the material, and I want to help other people learn it. Personally, I think it is criminal that they don't teach this to everyone because everyone could benefit. The second reason more people don't do it is time. Like I've been saying all along, time is the biggest asset you have. Most people, by the time they realize the necessity of saving for retirement, don't have as much time, maybe twenty or twenty-five years. Well, with those kinds of numbers, they'll struggle to get to $500,000. Now you can retire on less than $3 million, but it certainly doesn't hurt to have more. Except, perhaps, when it comes to taxes."

Mr. Sharp paused and went over to his computer and pulled up a tax chart to display on the screen.

"This," he said, gesturing toward the whiteboard, "is a chart of current tax brackets for the United States." The chart started at 10 percent for single individuals making up to $9,950 and went all the way up to 37 percent for individuals making $523,601 or more.

2021 Federal Income Tax Brackets and Rates for Single Filers, Married Couples Filing Jointly, and Heads of Households

Rate	For Single Individuals	For Married Individuals Filing Joint Returns	For Heads of Households
10%	Up to $9,950	Up to $19,900	Up to $14,200
12%	$9,951 to $40,525	$19,901 to $81,050	$14,201 to $54,200
22%	$40,526 to $86,375	$81,051 to $172,750	$54,201 to $86,350
24%	$86,376 to $164,925	$172,751 to $329,850	$86,351 to $164,900
32%	$164,926 to $209,425	$329,851 to $418,850	$164,901 to $209,400
35%	$209,426 to $523,600	$418,851 to $628,300	$209,401 to $523,600
37%	$523,601 or more	$628,301 or more	$523,601 or more

Source: Internal Revenue Service

"When you file your taxes, the amount of money you earned, after deductions, is what determines how much tax you pay. The more money you make, the more you pay in taxes. So even though those numbers in the investment account look pretty good, you have to factor in taxes and keep in mind that taxes will most likely go up by the time you reach retirement age."

"So, what, there will be like no money left for me after I pay the government?" Andrew asked.

"Well, it might feel like it at times. If you look at the chart, you pay the associated percentage rate up to the amounts specified. If you, as an individual, earned $40,000 of taxable income, you would pay 12 percent in taxes. If you earned $50,000, you'd pay the 12 percent up to $40,525 and then you'd pay 22 percent on the remaining $9,475."

"That's still a lot of money to pay in taxes."

"It is, but that's where careful planning and strategizing comes in. The whole point of long-term investing is that you don't plan on using the money for a long time. If you are willing to wait until you turn fifty-nine and a half before you touch it, you can open what is possibly the greatest investment account ever created: a Roth IRA."

"IRA—I've heard of that before. I think my parents have one."

"There are two main types of IRAs—Roth IRA and traditional IRA. With a traditional IRA, the money you put in can be deducted from what you pay in taxes. For instance, if you put $5,000 into your traditional IRA, then you don't pay taxes on that $5,000, which saves you, in the short run, about $500 to $1,000 depending on your tax bracket."

"That's a good deal," Andrew said. "What's the catch?"

"Ah, cynicism," said Mr. Sharp, smiling. "The catch is that when you withdraw it, once you retire right around age sixty, you have to pay taxes on all the money you take out. Let's say you take out $45,000 for living expenses when you retire. Now that $45,000 is taxed as if you just earned it that year so you pay whatever the current tax amount is. Let's say by then, the tax bracket you are in is 20 percent. That means that out of that $45,000, $9,000 is going to the government."

"But that's ridiculous—it's my money! I already earned it and invested it; why do I have to pay taxes on it again?"

"That's the thing—you didn't pay taxes on it the first

time. It was put in before taxes and you got the benefit up front. The cost comes later when you take the money out."

"Sounds pretty stupid to me," Andrew said.

"Stupid or not, Uncle Sam has to have his due. We're not going to get into the why behind taxes right now, but it is a frustrating necessity that we must accept. The point of building wealth is to create a means whereby taxes are no longer such a constant frustration because you have enough saved up to handle them."

"So, what's the other one?" Andrew asked. "The other IRA you were talking about."

"The Roth IRA—that's where things really get cool. With a Roth IRA, you put money in that has already been taxed. No special tax benefit up front, just money you've earned that has passed through your paycheck. But then, all that money grows tax-free. The entire time. Until you take it out, after you turn fifty-nine and a half, that money grows and grows and the compound interest compounds and compounds and you do not pay taxes on any of it. When you pull it out, it is yours without having to pay the government a dime."

"Wait, no catch?"

"Well, you defer your benefit. What I mean is you don't get the tax benefit up front—you have to pay taxes on that money. But when that money grows and grows and grows, you don't pay taxes on any of the interest. Basically, by skipping the short-term benefit, you reap massive benefits down the road. There are some basic rules to know about the account, but once people understand the ins and outs, the Roth IRA comes out as the real winner.

"The government knows this and that's why they limit how much you can put in each year. Right now, you can only put in up to $6,000 a year, or $500 a month. And while you can technically withdraw your contributions at any point, I don't recommend it as you'll only be hurting the future growth of your account. The earnings, or compound interest, cannot be touched until you reach fifty-nine and half years old or you are hit with penalties and interest that make it completely not worth it."

"Am I allowed to open one at my age? I mean, I don't even have a driver's license yet," Andrew said.

"As long as you can prove earned income, you can open a Roth IRA. A five-year-old can even open one if he/she can prove earned income. Since you have a job and are getting a paycheck, you can definitely open one as long as you don't exceed two numbers: The first is the amount you earned in a year. If you only made $2,000, you can't put in more than that. The second is the federal limit I just mentioned of $6,000 a year."

"So, a Roth IRA is a retirement account where I can't touch the earnings until I retire but when I do, I don't pay taxes on the earnings. If I had just a regular account, like one that isn't for retirement, I would pay taxes when I take the money out?"

"Taxes on the earnings, yes," said Mr. Sharp. "I know it is hard to think about your retirement when you are fifteen years old, but it is so important to start thinking about it because of the extra time it buys you in the end. Based on the charts we just looked at, if you wait until you are twenty-five to start saving but follow the same plan of saving $250 a month until you turn sixty-five, you would lose out on $2 million. By acting now, as a fifteen-year-old, you make a lot more money in the end."

"I always thought that your retirement was taken care of when you got a job, that your job gave you a retirement plan or something."

"Many jobs do," said Mr. Sharp. "In fact, many jobs offer a retirement matching program. After you graduate from college and land a job, chances are your employer will offer a dollar-for-dollar matching up to 3 percent of your income. Some have programs where they match fifty cents on the dollar up to 6 percent, which is the same as a 3 percent matching."

"But I shouldn't do that because I am doing the Roth IRA?"

"I advise you to do both. When employers offer any kind of retirement matching, it is smart to take them up on it because it is basically free money and you should always look for opportunities for free money—like that checking account promotion I sent you. Did you get that squared away?"

"Yes, and the money has already been deposited," said Andrew.

"I love it when it works like that. An employer offering retirement matching is much the same. The tax side works out a little differently, though. In that sense, most of those programs are similar to a traditional IRA, which is to say that the money you put in is pre-taxed, or money that you earn but don't pay taxes on."

"But I thought that wasn't as good as paying the taxes now to save later," said Andrew.

"I don't believe it is, but the benefit of getting the matching from your employer makes it worth it. Here's the plan I recommend to most people. First, find out what your employer offers in terms of matching. Then withhold whatever amount is necessary to meet that matching—if they match dollar for dollar up to 3 percent, then withhold 3 percent; if they match fifty cents on the dollar up to 6 percent, then withhold 6 percent. Get every scrap of dollar that they are willing to send your way. It's free money, after all. If you make $50,000 a year at your job and your employer matches up to 3 percent, that is $1,500 each year the company will give you. Let's assume that you work there for thirty years and never get a raise—obviously you'll get raises and grow your income, but for our purposes, let's say it stays the same. After thirty years, with the compound interest, that's $362,000 your company is giving you *for free.*"

"Why doesn't everyone do it if it is that much money?"

"Again, they don't know. Or they think, 'I can't afford to;

I need the money now.' That kind of thinking will keep people poor or living paycheck to paycheck their whole lives. When I counsel adults about finance, I always say 'Enroll in your employer's retirement matching program immediately.' If they say, 'I can't afford to,' I always say, 'You can't afford not to.' After they see the numbers, they usually come around.

"After you've set up your retirement matching, you are ready for the second step—putting as much as you can into your Roth IRA. Once you are in a place where you can afford it, try to max out that $6,000 contribution every year. There's a reason the government puts that limit on it, and I believe that you should take advantage of every option you can to build your financial freedom."

"So I should put in more than the $250 a month we looked at?"

"When you can afford it. By no means should you do that now—now is about getting into the habit of regularly contributing, every month. The easiest way to do that is to automate it. Once you set up a Roth IRA, you can automatically deposit $250 from your checking account every month. Set it up and let it run without you having to do it every time. Eventually you'll be able to afford to contribute more, and when that happens, hit your yearly maximum in your Roth IRA. If you hit your employer-matching number and then your yearly maximum and you can still save, then go back to your employer plan and contribute more. While the tax savings is not as great as the Roth IRA, it is still a tax savings and has a significant benefit. Look at these numbers," Mr. Sharp said.

By this point, Andrew's head was swimming with numbers and charts and calculations. Everything was starting to blur together, and he was losing sight of what Mr. Sharp was saying.

"Andrew? You still with me?"

"Yeah, sorry, I just zoned out a bit."

"It's a lot, I know," said Mr. Sharp. "Let me go over this last bit and then we'll break for the day."

"OK, sounds good," said Andrew.

"Let's say that by age thirty, you are married, and you have a job that pays $60,000 a year. Your partner also has a job that pays $60,000 a year. You bring in a combined gross income of $120,000 a year. You can claim a married couple filing jointly standard deduction of about $25,000, which takes your taxable income total down to about $95,000. There are other deductions that we won't get into today, but assuming tax brackets are similar to what they are now, you would owe $9,235 in federal taxes and then an additional 22 percent of everything you earned over $80,250."

Andrew's eyes began to glaze over once again.

"Try to stay with me; this is important," said Mr. Sharp. "The point is to get your taxable income as low as possible so that you don't pay as much in taxes. Money saved is money earned. If you earned $95,000, then you'll have to pay 22 percent of about $15,000, which"—Mr. Sharp got out his calculator and began typing in numbers—"is $3,300. That brings your total tax bill to right around $12,500. That's a hefty amount."

"Wait, I would have to pay over $12,000 in taxes?"

"Welcome to the lovely world of adulthood. The more you earn, the more you pay in taxes. Pure and simple."

"Then it doesn't pay to make more. Is there even a point to trying to earn more money?"

"The point is to be smart with your money so that you can pay as few taxes as possible while still giving Uncle Sam his due. Here's where the retirement contributions kick in. Remember how much you can contribute each year to your Roth IRA?"

"That's $6,000."

"Good. Well, with an employer plan, like a 401(k), you can contribute up to $19,500. So let's say your employer matches fifty cents on the dollar up to 6 percent of your salary. Well, if you are making $60,000 a year, then 6 percent is $3,600. Now here's the real way to think about that money: Every dollar you earn is really just seventy-eight cents. That's because the first twenty-two cents is given to the government. When you contribute to your 401(k), however, you keep the whole dollar. Giving a dollar to your retirement is actually giving more than a dollar, at least in the sense that you don't lose the 22 percent when you do it."

"I'm confused," Andrew said.

"Think about it like this," said Mr. Sharp. "Here are four quarters."

He laid out four quarters on the table in front of Andrew.

"Now, let's pretend you just finished working and these four quarters are yours. You have a choice to make—you can give me one quarter and keep three to spend on whatever you want." Mr. Sharp took one quarter and pushed the rest toward Andrew. "Or you can keep all four if you agree to put it into an account you can't touch until you turn fifty-nine and a half. Your choice: keep all or keep three."

"I obviously want to keep all," Andrew said.

"Precisely. And every dollar you contribute to your 401(k) lets you do that. Until you go to withdraw it, of course, but by then you'll have quite the Roth IRA saved up in another account and you can use the 401(k) to just supplement your income at that point."

"OK, I think I get it now," said Andrew. "The 401(k) operates similar to the Roth in that I can't touch it until I hit retirement age of fifty-nine and a half but, while one grows tax-free, the other goes in tax-free."

"That's the basic gist. You'll be allowed to withdraw your Roth contributions at any point, just not the earnings."

"Meaning?" asked Andrew.

"Meaning that any money you put into your Roth has already been taxed, so it is free to take out at any point. The interest and compound interest, however, has not been taxed, so it all has to stay in until age fifty-nine and a half."

"OK," said Andrew. "So, if I did both, like you are saying, how much would I have when I retire?"

"Let's see—we're going to run two calculations. The first will be if you retire at age fifty-nine and a half and the second if you retire at age sixty-five."

Mr. Sharp erased the whiteboard and drew a line down the center. On one side of the line, he wrote "59½" and on the other side, he wrote "65." He then pulled up the interest calculator website and started punching in numbers.

"Keep in mind, we have a few assumptions," he said as he was typing. "Assumption one is that you are earning 10 percent in interest—again, we will cover how to do that next class. Assumption two is that you are starting now and using our $250 a month savings plan until you hit age twenty-five, where you increase it to $6,000 a year, or $500 a month. Assumption three is that you get a job at age twenty-four making $35,000 that gives you a 3 percent matching on your retirement and you take advantage of that from the start. Assumption four is that by age thirty, you are contributing a full 10 percent of a now $60,000 salary with the 3 percent matching and hitting the $6,000 a year in your Roth IRA."

"Uh, that's a lot to take in," Andrew said.

"Agreed. It makes sense, though, right? I just wanted to go over all the assumptions before we start running numbers, so it makes sense and we're not just making things up. Now let's see what we get."

Mr. Sharp spent the next few minutes putting in a series

of numbers and jotting down calculations on a sheet of paper. Finally, he stopped and examined his work.

"That's more than I thought," he said, with a wide grin on his face.

"What is it? Tell me!" said Andrew, brimming with impatience.

Mr. Sharp went to the board and wrote, under the 59½ column, $3.5 million. Then he went to the 65 column and wrote $6.4 million.

"Wow, $6.4 million!" Andrew said, his voice rising with enthusiasm. "You've got to be kidding me!"

"And the crazy thing," Mr. Sharp said, "is that we calculated that based on just your salary and based on you never earning more than $60,000 a year. This is not based on someone making $250,000 a year or something crazy like that. You could make a basically average wage and still retire as a multimillionaire. Heck, retire with over $6 million."

"I don't even know how I would spend that much money," Andrew said. "I mean, don't get me wrong, I'm sure I could, but still, that's crazy!"

"It is crazy, and it's all because you have the element of time on your side. Now I promised to get you out of here before your head exploded, but hopefully, I've at least convinced you to look into opening a Roth IRA in the near future."

"Near future?" Andrew asked. "How about right now? This is unbelievable! I'm going to talk to my parents about it tonight."

"And more power to you, Andrew," said Mr. Sharp. "I have to say this has been as much fun for me as it has been for you, and I don't even have the element of time on my side anymore. I followed a similar plan starting at your age, and I am still shocked about how it has all added up. It's amazing to see what you can do when you start early."

Andrew got out his phone to take a picture of the whiteboard.

"Wait until my parents see this—they are going to flip out."

"I look forward to hearing all about it. For now, though, I'm going to let you go and next time we meet, we will get a little deeper into how to earn that 10 percent I keep talking about."

"Sounds good, Mr. Sharp, thanks!" Andrew said, getting up to leave. "Holy smoke, I'm going to be loaded when I retire!"

"Yes," said Mr. Sharp, "I do believe you will be."

CHAPTER NINE
INVESTING AND RATE OF RETURN

With the flurry of activity around preparing for midterm exams, getting in a few shifts at work, and celebrating his sixteenth birthday, the time seemed to fly by before Andrew was once again in room 205. Mr. Sharp was, as usual, waiting for him while erasing the whiteboard.

"Good to see you, Andrew," said Mr. Sharp. "How's work going? Still implementing your ideas?"

"It's going really well. The other day Carol asked me to work with two of the other front of the house employees on how to interact with customers. The crazy thing is that both of them have worked there longer than I have."

"I see," said Mr. Sharp. "How did they feel about having to take a lesson from you?"

"Honestly it was a little awkward at first, but I think they came around when they saw that I genuinely enjoy talking to the customers. By the end, they were just as excited as I was—we even made a competition out of it to see who could make a customer smile or laugh just by us saying 'Make it an awesome day!'"

"It's great that they are giving you more responsibility," Mr. Sharp said. "Just keep in mind that as you rise up in the ranks, there will be those who get pretty jealous and may not have your best interests at heart."

"It's funny you say that," Andrew said, "because I was thinking that about Steve. The other day I overheard him talking to Dan and saying something about how he was tired of hearing my name. I didn't hear the whole conversation because he saw me and his expression changed to a smile, but I could tell it wasn't genuine."

"It wouldn't surprise me at all if Steve was frustrated with you. After all, he just wanted you to play the game and keep your head low. I'm proud of you, though, and I imagine your parents must be, too. Have you been able to find a balance with schoolwork in the midst of all of this?"

"I think so," said Andrew. "Now that cross country is over and I'm not playing a winter sport, I've had more time. I also decided to give up the National Honor Society this year. My mom wasn't too sure about giving it up, but I think it was the right decision. It may look good on a college resume, but it was a big time-suck."

"Sounds to me like you are prioritizing," said Mr. Sharp.

"I'm starting to get the hang of it. I've even gotten to spend time with Kevin—he got a job at Gap, so I get to see him quite a bit now on breaks. We even carpool together some nights."

"That's great!" said Mr. Sharp. "I'm glad you're finding time for your friends."

"And now down to business," said Andrew, smiling.

"Oh?" asked Mr. Sharp.

"I spent some time looking at all the numbers you went over on retirement, and I've decided that I want to start investing so I can work toward some of those big goals. I mean, $6 million is no joke."

"You know, Andrew, I'm glad you brought that up because I've also been thinking a lot about that, and I wanted to bring up a topic with you related to investing and making money. Let me start with a question—what would you say is the ultimate point of building wealth?"

"The ultimate point?" Andrew asked. "To have money, I guess. To buy whatever I want."

Mr. Sharp looked at Andrew without replying.

"OK, well, I guess maybe the point," Andrew continued, "is to have the security that money brings. To not have to worry about being poor."

"A valid reason, certainly," said Mr. Sharp. "I do wonder, though, if there is some higher reason or larger purpose to it. If it is just to have security, that security could be achieved with far less."

"So, like, why $6 million if you could live on a lot less?"

"Exactly," said Mr. Sharp. "Let's say that you set the long-term goal of building your wealth like we outlined last class. You save and you invest and your account grows until it is far more than you could spend in your lifetime. What then? Is it just about being rich?"

"Being rich certainly would be nice," said Andrew.

"And there's nothing wrong with that, necessarily," said Mr. Sharp.

"But I don't know—are you trying to get me to say something about giving money away to charity or a higher purpose or something?

"Not entirely," said Mr. Sharp. "I simply want you to begin to think of the obtaining of wealth not as an end in and of itself. There are plenty of stories of people who spend their lives seeking riches only to lose everything of true value in the process. Are you familiar with the famous film *Citizen Kane*?"

"We watched it in class last year," Andrew said. "I was the only one who liked it—everyone else said it was boring."

"You see, I said before that you had good taste," said Mr. Sharp, smiling. "I also like that film. Very much, in fact. To me, it is the quintessential American story: A man builds an empire for himself and attains what seems to be greatness in the form of wealth and power. Yet he dies miserable and alone longing for the one thing he had to give up to attain it all."

"Rosebud."

"Yes, Rosebud. The symbol of his stolen childhood. The sled that represents his lost youth. He built up his wealth his whole life at the cost of his youth and his family and his loved ones. In the end, he had all the money in the world but no one to love and no one to love him. One might suggest he died poorer than most.

"You see, that's the thing, Andrew. I don't want you to become so obsessed with earning wealth that you lose sight of the things that really matter. Learning about money is certainly exciting; I mean, I've dedicated a large part of my life studying it and being fascinated by it, but I have to remind myself that it is not everything, not by a long shot. If we become obsessed with earning money for money's sake, then we risk alienating the people who really matter. For me, the whole point of investing and building wealth has been not for the sake of having money but for the sake of being able to use that money to help other people accomplish their dreams."

"So this *is* about charity, then," Andrew said.

"Not charity as much as having the freedom to follow your passions. I am passionate about young entrepreneurs and helping people who are trying to launch business concepts. I myself am an entrepreneur, and I know how hard it is to get an idea off the ground. If I can afford to help others, then that enables me to put my wealth to work while making a difference."

"Like your Why," Andrew said.

"Hmm?" asked Mr. Sharp.

"Your Why. Like you said in class the other day when you were talking about how companies had to have a Why. The

Simon Sinek thing. Your Why is helping entrepreneurs."

"You're exactly right. It's not just companies that have a Why; it's also individuals. That's why a company, if its Why matches the Why of an individual, gains a customer for life. But you have to know your Why, which starts by having one in the first place. Think of it as a guiding reason. If someone asked me why I am so interested in making and investing money, I would say it is because good intentions can only go so far. If I want to make a meaningful difference in the world, it takes money to do it. If you can get ahead of the system and earn money, you can put that to use to make the world a better place. I realize it sounds cheesy—"

"No, actually, it makes a lot of sense," Andrew said. "When I went home the other day, I was wondering what I would do with $6 million, and other than having a cool house and car and nice clothes and everything, I didn't know what I would do with it. I was wondering what the point would be to working so long to make that much money to just spend it on stuff."

"Andrew, you are speaking with a wisdom far beyond your years," Mr. Sharp said. "And I don't want to harp on the point too much, but I just want you to consider what a difference you can make in the world with your money rather than just worry about it accumulating. After all, many people far wiser than me have pointed out that a life spent making the world a better place is a life far from wasted.

"Anyway," continued Mr. Sharp, "Let's get into the topic

for today. We talked through the strategies for planning for retirement last class, and we talked more about the amazing power of compound interest. All of our factoring has been with the assumption that we are earning a 10 percent rate of return with our money, and today we're going to examine how that is possible. To start, what can you tell me about the stock market?"

"The stock market," Andrew said, taking a deep breath. "The stock market. Well, the stock market is basically where you can buy part of a business, right? Like you can buy a share in a company, and then if that company does well, your share price goes up?"

"Right on the money," said Mr. Sharp. "Any companies in particular you know in the stock market?"

"I know Amazon and Apple are big," said Andrew. "My dad always talks about P&G and how they are a blue something."

"Blue chip—a big company with a solid, long-standing reputation."

"Yes, that," said Andrew. "That's about it. I know the stock market is risky and a lot of people have lost money in it."

"Well let's set the record straight about some of it. First, I want to explain a key difference when it comes to stocks. There are individual stocks for individual companies, like Apple or Amazon or P&G. When you buy those stocks, you are, like you said, buying a share of a company and if that company does well, you do well, and if they don't, well, you also take a loss. Buying individual stocks is certainly risky and the risk only intensifies the more you invest. So, if you put all of your money in a single company stock and then that company has a bad sales report or some crazy news story comes out that destroys the company, then you lose everything. Stories that circulate about situations like that are what cause people to fear the stock market.

"Another way to buy stocks, however, is to invest in an index fund. Have you heard the name 'S&P 500' or 'Dow Jones' before?"

Andrew nodded.

"You've probably heard it along the lines of someone on the news saying, 'The Dow is down forty points today.' Am I safe to assume you don't know what that means?"

Andrew nodded again.

"Fair enough, and the truth is, most people don't. Let me break it down like this."

Mr. Sharp went to the board and wrote "US Stock Market" at the top and then drew two large circles in the middle of the board. On the left circle, he wrote "Dow Jones," and on the right one, he wrote "S&P."

"Here's your crash course: These are two popular indices in the US stock market—the Dow Jones Industrial Average and the Standard and Poor's 500 Index. Think of these not as individual companies but as collections of companies. Are you familiar with the word *microcosm*?"

"I've heard it before but don't know what it means," Andrew said.

"It's like a 'small world.' A scale or a model. In other words, a microcosm is a small thing that captures, in miniature, the larger thing it is representing. Both indices, the Dow Jones and the S&P, are a composite of the US stock market. Picture a picnic basket—inside that basket, you don't just have one item; you have sandwiches, drinks, napkins, silverware, and desserts. That's how these index funds work—inside each you have a collection of multiple companies rather than a single one. You with me?"

"I think so," said Andrew.

"Explain it back to me if you can," said Mr. Sharp.

"Each circle drawn on the board represents a collection of companies in the United States that moves as a whole."

"That's the right idea," said Mr. Sharp. "Let's start with the Dow. It is a collection of thirty companies, large ones, like Nike, Verizon, Home Depot, and Coca-Cola. If just one company has a bad day, it doesn't mess up the whole index too much because there are twenty-nine other companies to look at. The companies represent all sorts of different industries, or 'sectors,' like technology, consumer goods, oil and gas, health care, and so on. The Dow is supposed to represent an overall picture of the stock market, but since it is just thirty companies, the picture is quite narrow."

"How many companies are in the stock market?"

"The number varies," said Mr. Sharp, "between the high,

back in the late 1990s, of around 8,000 companies, to much lower, as of 2016, of around 3,600 companies. The New York Stock Exchange, which is the biggest one in the world, has close to 3,000 public companies listed."

"Three thousand?" Andrew asked. "So, thirty is just, what, like a percentage of that?"

"You're dead right—exactly 1 percent. But keep in mind that these are major, established companies. Something else, though not that important right now at the risk of confusing you, is that the Dow Jones is 'price-weighted,' which means that companies with higher share prices have a larger effect on the index than ones with small prices."

Mr. Sharp went to the whiteboard and wrote "market capitalization" in large letters under the two circles.

"Market capitalization," he said, "is how many shares a company has multiplied by the share price. If a company's shares are thirty-five dollars each and it has two million shares in circulation, then its market cap is seventy million."

"Would that make it one of the biggest?" Andrew asked.

"Not quite," said Mr. Sharp. "Take a company like Apple or Amazon—they have market caps of over a trillion dollars. Not billion, but trillion. Roughly anything over two hundred billion is considered mega cap and anything over about ten billion is big cap. That $70-million company is definitely small cap.

"Back to the Dow Jones—some investors, myself included, feel that the Dow is not the best reflection of the overall market because it focuses on the price of the stock instead of the market capitalization of the stock."

"Why are some stocks priced lower if the company is worth more?"

"Because as a company grows, it may periodically decide to split the stocks, which means that if you own one share, the price gets divided in half and you now own two shares but at half the value each. Same total price but double the shares. There are several reasons companies do this but often it is to make their share price more attractive to buyers."

"Does a company have to split their stock?"

"No, they don't. Warren Buffett, widely considered to be the greatest investor of all time, runs a company called Berkshire Hathaway and they have never split their stock. Get this—when they first went public, which means when they first started selling stock for people to buy, the shares were $7.60 per share. Now they are well over $400,000 per share."

"Wait," said Andrew. "Does that mean that if you originally bought it in—when was it first offered—"

"In the early 1960s," interjected Mr. Sharp.

"If you bought it for $7.60 in the 1960s, then it would be worth $400,000 today?"

"Even more, but yes."

"Just to clarify, if I bought one hundred shares back then it would have only cost $760, and today it would be worth ..." Andrew got out his phone and opened the calculator and started typing numbers, "$40 million. What!"

"That's the beauty of the stock market. And also the frustration—who had the foresight to know back then what it would become? But, again, that's single stock investing, and we are talking about the larger index funds. While the Dow focuses on price, other indices, like the second one here, the Standard and Poor 500, or S&P 500, look at the market capitalization of the companies. The other advantage to the S&P 500 is that it is a collection of five hundred companies instead of thirty. Specifically, it is the five-hundred-largest-traded companies in the United States, which is a much better reflection of the overall US stock market.

"Can you buy shares in these large index funds? Like could I buy a share of Dow or a share of the S&P 500?"

"You're beating me to the punch," said Mr. Sharp. "You absolutely can. That's the beauty of index funds—you are not buying just one stock and putting your eggs in one basket. For every one of the Warren Buffett companies, there are hundreds of companies where you would have lost all your money had you invested everything in them. With an index fund, you are buying a stake in all five hundred companies. Not a share, per se, as some of these companies have incredibly expensive shares, but a stake. You are buying a portion of each company. This way, if one company just tanks, you aren't at risk of losing everything. Instead, you own a collective piece of all of them and this makes your investment less risky, especially when it comes to long-term investing."

"Are companies like Apple and Amazon in the S&P 500?" asked Andrew.

"Yes, they are, along with quite a few others. Each year about a dozen or so companies start to fail, and they get replaced with others so that each year it is an assembled group of 'winners.' As a result, over a long period of time, an investment in an index fund that tracks the S&P 500 tends to earn a steady return. The S&P 500 has been around since the 1920s, but it did not have five hundred companies until 1957. If you look at the rate of returns from 1957 until now, you get an average of around 10 percent. That means if you did nothing other than put your money in a fund that tracks the S&P 500 and left it alone, you'd get about 10 percent year after year."

"If someone had put in $1,000 in 1957, what would it be worth today?" Andrew asked.

"Ha, your brain works like mine," said Mr. Sharp. "Let's see …" He got out his interest calculator and punched in the numbers. "A $1,000 investment in 1957 until today with 10 percent average rate of return equals"—he paused to double-check his numbers—"just under $450,000."

"Wow—and it only takes $1,000 and sixty-four years."

"Yes, sixty-four years. But think of how much sooner you'd reach that amount if you kept adding to the initial investment of $1,000," said Mr. Sharp. "Now, if you look at just the last ten years of the S&P 500, you'll see that returns averaged closer to 13 percent. The fact of the matter is we have no idea what the next ten, twenty, or fifty years in the stock market will look like, but by investing in an index fund that tracks something like the S&P 500, you'll have a better chance of earning those higher returns. You could even invest in a fund that tracks the entire US stock market—all the publicly traded companies. This is an even more diversified fund and it averages a return around 10 percent over the long term."

"So how is that better than investing in a company like Apple or Amazon when it is early on, and you can make a ton of money?"

"You're right that if you had invested in Apple or Amazon in the '90s, you'd be sitting fine right now. But you would have gone through some serious bumps in the road. Have you heard of the 'dot-com crash'?"

Andrew shook his head.

"The dot-com crash happened in 2000 because of the crazy rise in Internet-related companies. There's a whole history behind how it happened but suffice to say that if you'd had your money in Apple, you would have lost 50 percent in a single day and if you had it in Amazon, you would have lost 90 percent. Most people pulled out of those stocks and took their losses because they didn't have the foresight to see what the companies would become. And who could blame them? Imagine saving all your life to lose 90 percent of it in one year. That's why individual companies can be risky."

"What happened to the S&P 500 during the dot-com crash?" Andrew asked.

"It suffered but not as much as the individual companies. At its low, in 2002, it dropped over 23 percent. The next year, however, it was up 26 percent. The key is to think of it as long term by averaging the returns. Some years your account will lose money—that's the nature of the stock market. But the long-term trend is upward, and if you are investing for the long term, index funds are the way to go."

"So, I should just put my money in the S&P 500 and leave it?"

"That's one strategy," said Mr. Sharp. "And a pretty good one at that. In fact, since we already mentioned Warren Buffett, he once won a famous million-dollar bet by betting that the S&P 500 would beat a series of investment selections made by highly paid professionals. He said that over ten years, the S&P 500 would beat the so-called best and brightest minds on Wall Street. Long story short, he won. By a landslide. There are ways, however, to be even more strategic. We're not going to get into the weeds with those right now because you're just getting started, but if you take a serious interest in investing and in the stock market, there are some resources I'll recommend to help you make smart decisions."

"So how do you buy an index fund?"

"It's the same way you would buy shares of an individual company. You use an online broker, and you look up the ticker or stock symbol. Apple, for example, is listed as 'AAPL' while Amazon is listed as 'AMZN.' Once you find the index fund you are interested in, you buy shares equivalent to whatever money you are investing," said Mr. Sharp.

"If I have a Roth IRA like we talked about, can that be invested in these funds?" Andrew asked.

"You have a few options with that," Mr. Sharp said. "When you open a Roth IRA, you are basically opening an account that can then be invested in the stock market. You can have a financial advisor invest it for you at the cost of a percentage of the money taken each year. Or, and my preferred way, you can do it yourself, by picking the funds you want to invest in and then that money is sitting in that account but invested in what you chose. So, if you want to just put it all into an index fund that tracks the S&P 500, or one of these other indices, then you do that. I don't recommend filling it with individual stocks. The whole point of the index fund is you are creating diversity. Have you ever heard someone talk about having a 'diverse stock portfolio'?"

Andrew nodded.

"That's what they mean—don't just buy a few individual stocks, but spread your investments around—have a plan. If you want to get a little more involved in strategy, you could do something like this ..." Mr. Sharp hooked his laptop up to the projector and displayed a triangle chart detailing percentages and categories.

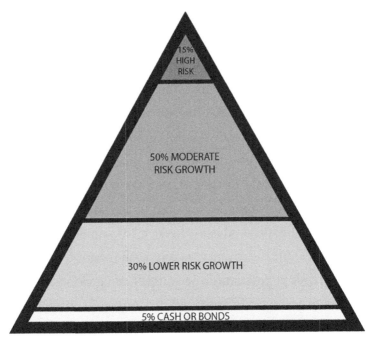

"This is an investment pyramid," said Mr. Sharp. "It is broken into ages so that the younger you are, the riskier your investments can afford to be because you have the best asset of all on your side."

"Time," Andrew said, smiling.

"Time indeed. Look here," Mr. Sharp said, pointing to the chart. "The pyramid reflects your portfolio. Your portfolio is basically all the money in your account and how it is dispersed. Since you are a teenager, you could invest between 10 and 15 percent of your portfolio in what's called an 'aggressive growth' category, something that is high risk. Don't put all your portfolio in it as that would be a mistake, but you can put up to 15 percent in. Next you put 50 percent into a category that is moderate/high risk or 'growth'—a category like a good index fund. Thirty percent of your portfolio goes into a lower risk investment and the remaining 5 percent goes into conventional bonds or cash or a mix of both."

"Bonds?" Andrew asked. "What are bonds?"

"Think of a conventional bond as a loan," said Mr. Sharp, "but in this case, you are giving the loan to an investor, like the government or a corporation. In return for the loan, you are paid interest on that money. If a company is trying to raise money, it may sell a bond for $500 and offer 5 percent interest for five years. Here's what that means ..."

Mr. Sharp began writing the numbers on the whiteboard.

"You give them $500 and each year, for five years, you get $25 in interest. Then, at the end of the five years, you get your $500 back. Therefore, your total return is $625 for a five-year investment of $500. It's certainly not 12 percent, which would have brought back $800 after five years. Compound interest doesn't play a part in conventional bonds, but they are considered safer and far less risky than stocks. I certainly wouldn't recommend your whole portfolio be made up of bonds, but they certainly help for those who want less volatility, or fluctuation, in their portfolio. Slow and steady, as it were."

"It sounds like a savings bond. My grandpa gave me one for Christmas a few years ago."

"Same kind of idea—those are backed by the US Treasury

and they are guaranteed by the federal government. Lower interest rates but super safe investments."

"So should I just put everything in a stock fund like the S&P 500 like you said, or should I break it up into these categories?"

"That's where your personal choice comes in. The general rule to consider is that you want the highest rate of return you can get without going above your risk tolerance. Some people recommend a mix of stocks and bonds, which is certainly one way to go. All along, I've been suggesting that we calculate our investments using an expected 10 percent rate of return. I believe that's justifiable simply because it's the historical average of the S&P 500. But there are no guarantees when it comes to the stock market—hence the overall risk. What I recommend is that you find a strategy that works for you, and you stick with it. With a clear strategy, you have a better chance of meeting your goals."

"Goals again—everything comes down to goals," Andrew said.

"That's true," said Mr. Sharp. "Have you been listening to *The Magic of Thinking Big* like I asked?"

"We're halfway through," Andrew said. "I think my parents are getting into it even more than me. They're coming up with all of these goals for our family, and they've even got a chart on the fridge about it."

"How about you? Any insights?"

"Well, yesterday driving home, we heard the story about the bricklayers."

"Remind me what that story was," said Mr. Sharp.

"OK, well, there are these three bricklayers and they are, obviously, laying bricks down. And someone comes up and asks the first one what he's doing and he says, 'I'm just laying these bricks.' The person goes up to the second one and the second one says, 'I'm getting ten bucks an hour; that's what I'm doing.' When the person goes to the third one, the third one says, 'I'm building the world's best building.'"

"I love that story," said Mr. Sharp.

"Yeah—I thought of you when I heard it. It sounds like something you would say."

"Ha—I guess you've got me figured out. The third bricklayer saw the bigger picture—he viewed his work as important. He's going to go places. Even if he remains a bricklayer, he's going to be the best bricklayer the company ever had because he understands the Why. I'm guessing you thought about applying that to what you are doing at The Twist?"

"I did, yes. When I first started, I was doing it for twelve dollars an hour, just selling soft pretzels. Now I'm giving customers a good experience while they are walking around the mall. I'm trying to make their visit to the store their best experience of the day. And it is so much fun."

"And just like the bricklayer in the story, I imagine that will lead to more and more responsibility for you," said Mr. Sharp. "And maybe even that raise you are working toward."

"You know, it's funny," Andrew said. "I've kind of

forgotten about that the last few times I've been at work. I mean, sure, I'd like to get paid more and all, but I'm not thinking about it every second while I'm at work."

Mr. Sharp folded his arms across his chest and smiled.

"You know, Andrew," he said, "sometimes I find it hard to believe you are only a sophomore in high school."

Mr. Sharp sat down and let out a big sigh. He looked over at Andrew, whose face showed a mixture of exhaustion and excitement.

"Well, Andrew, I think that wraps up class today—I think you have quite a bit to mull over in the next few days."

"Yes, as usual," said Andrew, smiling.

CHAPTER TEN

DECISIONS, DECISIONS

"Andrew, there's someone I'd like you to meet."

Andrew looked up from his spreadsheet where he had been updating the current stock supply on items at the front of the house. The spreadsheet idea had taken off and he was able, in just a few minutes each shift, to calculate all the stock needs for The Twist and anticipate any shortages before they became a problem.

When he looked up, he saw that Carol was standing by the register with two slightly older and well-dressed people who looked out of place in the soft-pretzel store.

"Hi, Carol, sure, let me just save this." Andrew pressed save and put his computer to sleep.

"Let's talk in the back," Carol said, leading the way to her office in the back of the store. Andrew followed with the two individuals bringing up the rear. He couldn't help but feel that he was swept up in an official procession of people as they wove through the small store.

"Have a seat," Carol said, gesturing to two chairs placed

in front of the desk. Andrew sat in one and Carol sat down next to him. The two new people made their way to the other side of the desk and sat down facing Carol and Andrew.

"Andrew, we have heard a lot about you," the man said. He appeared to be in his late sixties with mostly gray hair and a neatly trimmed beard. The distinguished woman, her dark hair bound tightly in a bun, slid into the neighboring chair, all the while smiling at Andrew.

"Carol here has told us that you have made quite a splash since you started here three months ago," she said, nodding toward Carol.

"Allow us to introduce ourselves," said the man. "Bob and Christy Roe. We happen to own this little establishment," he said, gesturing around him.

"Bob and Christy live in upstate New York," Carol said, "and they rarely get to visit the store, so I keep them informed of what happens on a regular basis."

"Which actually brings us to the purpose of our visit," said Bob. "Christy was going through the books, and we both thought we had found a mistake because sales for the last month are higher, and I mean significantly higher, than any of the last three years."

"Nothing against Carol," Christy said, smiling, "but we assumed that a few days had been counted twice or that some expenses had not been calculated. But when we double-checked everything with our accountant, it all came out correct. This past month, The Twist did 16 percent more business than any other November in the past."

"We immediately reached out to find out what was going on. The news was more shocking given the fact that we had started the process of shopping around to find a buyer for the business," Bob said, reaching out to hold Christy's hand. "Ten years of owning a soft-pretzel business had taught us that it can be more trouble than it's worth. Honestly, if it weren't for Carol here and how great she has been, we probably would have sold years ago."

Carol's face betrayed the slightest display of blushing as she smiled and turned her gaze downward to study the floor.

"Yes, Carol has been great," Christy said, "but with an independent business like this, there's always the temptation to sell to an operation that has multiple stores and operates franchises. All of this is beside the point, however, because once Carol explained how you had started ramping up excitement with customers, and then how she had asked you to work with the other employees on getting in on the excitement, we realized you were special."

"Normally it's just my parents who tell me that," Andrew said, smiling.

Everyone laughed and Andrew began to feel more at ease despite sitting a few feet from the people who owned the business where he worked.

"Tell us, Andrew," said Bob, "what's your story? What got into you to start kicking it up several notches here?"

"I suppose it started with this class I'm taking at school

where we are talking a lot about setting goals and thinking big. As an assignment, I had to listen to this audiobook called *The Magic of—*"

"*The Magic of Thinking Big?*" Bob asked. "By David Schwartz? A phenomenal book—I wish it was required reading for everyone."

"Honey, let him finish," Christy said.

"Of course, my apologies," Bob said.

"Well, I listened to the book and thought a lot about the goals in my life and how to think big about them. I even went home and made a chart that looked at all the areas like school and finances and work. Then I decided where I wanted to be with each one in a few months, a few years, and long term. A few of my goals started to blend together because in order to meet my financial goals, I had to increase my work, and so I started to focus on that in order to help fuel some of my other goals.

"So I sat down and really tried to think about what would help me do better at work. My teacher, Mr. Sharp, talked to me about figuring out the Why behind the business, like why do we sell pretzels in the first place."

"Interesting," said Bob who, after getting a glance from his wife, said, "I'm sorry, please continue."

"At first I thought the Why for the business was just to make money. But then I came around to realize that we are here to brighten the day for customers who are wandering through the mall. I figured that's why we were supposed to say 'Make it an awesome day.' Well, no one really says that, I mean ..." He shot a look at Carol who betrayed no surprise or emotion.

"It's OK, Andrew," said Christy. "Trust us; we know that it didn't really catch on."

"I just thought that if I really tried to say it and mean it and make customers feel like we cared, then it would help. I tried it a few times, and it seemed to make a difference."

"If I could interject," said Carol, "it did more than just make a difference. We have had dozens of customers come up and ask for Andrew by name during times when he's not present. He makes people smile and his energy is contagious—I asked him to work with a few others and now they are all in on it and it's like a whole new workplace. I haven't seen anything like it since you brought me on a few years ago. Andrew even helped me reorganize the stock list, and he's been taking on more and more responsibility. He never complains and always does his work to perfection."

"It reminds me of that saying," said Bob, "where if you want something done, you give it to a busy person. Andrew here sounds like quite the catch. How old are you?"

"I just turned sixteen," Andrew said. "I'm a sophomore in high school."

"Sixteen. Wow," said Bob. "I had you pegged for a few years older."

"He acts older than most of the eighteen- and nineteen-year-old students we have here," Carol said.

"Andrew, I'll cut to the chase," said Bob, leaning back in his chair. "We are impressed with what you've done in such a short time. We want to look into expanding your role here and giving you more influence overall."

"Really? That's great, I mean, sure!" said Andrew.

"I know that because you're still in school, you can't really ramp up your hours, at least during the school year, but I think we can work something out to your benefit. Are you aware of the role the different store managers play here?"

"I think so," said Andrew. "Carol seems to be the head manager and Dan and Steve are sort of lead managers when she's gone. They all handle counting down the cash drawer and scheduling people and things like that."

"Carol has been with us the longest," Bob said. "Dan started two years ago and Steve came last fall as a college freshman. We were trying to hire someone to help ease Carol's burden of running the store in our absence so we made them lead managers. They've done a fine job—"

Andrew caught a quick shadow of a frown on Carol's face when Bob said this.

"I can't say we've been thrilled with all of the results, but that's beside the point. Typically, to be a manager, you must be a full-time employee, but we did some digging and think we have a plan figured out that will be mutually beneficial."

"Andrew, how would you like to be our brand-new customer service and marketing manager?" Christy asked, with a big smile on her face.

"Seriously? I mean, wow, I don't know, what would that mean that I do?"

"You keep your current hours," Bob said, "and maybe during breaks from school, you pick up a few more shifts here and there. You work with the sales team like you have been on greeting customers and spreading enthusiasm. You think of ways to increase awareness about the business, like you did with your cards a while ago."

"You heard about those?" Andrew asked.

Bob reached into his pocket and pulled one out. "Pretty impressive for an employee who just started. And with no budget. I want to give you a monthly budget and see what you can do to increase our presence. The truth is, your energy has given me a revitalized vision for the company. I'm not in the market to sell anymore. In fact, Christy and I will be visiting more often, and we are going to come alongside to really help this business be all it can be. With your help and with Carol's leadership, I think we have some great things coming."

"Andrew, this position comes with an increase in pay," Christy said. "I understand you currently make twelve dollars an hour?"

"Yes, that's correct," Andrew said. His heart was racing— this was the moment he had been waiting for since making the goal chart at the start of the year. He silently crossed his fingers and hoped, beyond all measure, that he would get the one-dollar raise he had been working toward.

"Twelve dollars an hour is hardly a rate for a customer service and marketing manager," Bob said, smiling. "We're thinking of something with a little more of a perk. We also think that you just might be someone who is motivated differently than an hourly wage. If you are as goal-oriented as you say you are, then this might be right up your alley. Here's what we'd like to set up."

Bob pulled a folder out of his briefcase and opened it on the desk in front of Andrew. Inside were a series of charts and graphs in a range of colors.

"These are our sales, broken down by month, for the last three years. On this chart, you'll see where we were one year ago at this time for the month of November and here ..." Bob pointed to a chart with a line significantly higher, "here is where we are this November. As you can see, sales are up significantly."

"While there are a lot of variables to attribute that to," Christy said, "it is clear that you have made a big difference in just a few short months."

"This number here," said Bob, continuing, "is the total gross sales we had for last month. $34,800. Not too bad, although you have to consider that you have to pay for labor, rent, equipment loans, and product so after all that, the number is significantly lower. But with increased revenue, you have increased profits. And we believe that investing in you as a customer and marketing manager will bring in increased revenue."

Both Bob and Christy paused to look at Andrew, whose eyes were getting wider with each chart.

"Is this making sense?" Christy asked. "I hope we are not overwhelming you."

"It makes sense, yes," said Andrew. "It's just a lot to take in."

"I'll get to the point," Bob said. "We're going to give you an option, and there's no need to let us know right now what you decide—you can take a week and tell us your choice. Option one is a raise. We would like to start your new position at fifteen dollars an hour."

Bob paused to smile at Andrew's open-mouthed reaction.

"That's right," he said, continuing, "a 25 percent raise. Not bad, considering you've been here just three or four months. That's option one. Option two is a little more complicated. See if you can follow me here—last year, we had $30,000 in gross sales for the same month I just showed you. A 16 percent increase is a big deal, and what we would like to offer you is to keep your twelve-dollar-an-hour salary as a base pay and to take a percentage of the increased profits as your extra pay."

Andrew looked confused and Christy jumped in to help explain.

"In other words," she said, "you get a bonus if sales are higher than the previous year. Whatever that amount is, above and beyond the same month from last year, you get 5 percent of the gross sales."

"Do you have your phone on you?" Bob asked.

Andrew nodded.

"Go ahead and open your calculator. This month was $4,800 more than the same month last year so multiply $4,800 by .05 and let me know what you get."

"It's $240," Andrew said after calculating.

"That means that at the end of the month, you would get $240 as a bonus. On top of your twelve dollars an hour. Basically, we are offering a three dollar an hour raise or a profit-sharing option. Since you are working about fifteen hours a week and there's a little over four weeks in a month, or about thirty days, the three dollars an hour raise would work out to—"

"An extra $195 a month," Andrew said.

"I knew he was a smart one," Bob said, smiling at Christy.

"So you're saying that I can choose between fifteen dollars an hour or a percentage of the profits above where we were last year."

"Yes, your decision," Bob said. "And no need to let us know now—take some time to think about it. In the meantime," Bob pulled an envelope out of his briefcase, "take this as a small token of our appreciation."

After saying goodbye and shaking hands with Bob and Christy, Carol led Andrew back to the front of the store.

"How do you feel?" she asked. "Overwhelmed?"

"I'm pumped," he said, grinning up at her. "I'm super pumped."

After she returned to the back, Andrew opened the envelope and examined the contents. A post-it note that said "Thanks for your initiative" was stuck to the top of a check made payable to Andrew Black for $250.

The rest of his shift passed in a blur of disbelief and excitement. He was so energized that during his thirty-minute break, he walked down to Gap to visit Kevin and treat him to a triple-dip sundae at the food court.

"You know," Kevin said, in between mouthfuls of ice cream, "This new position of yours will be mutually beneficial."

"Oh yeah?" Andrew asked, laughing. "And just how is that?"

"Well, as your business manager—"

"That's a good one," said Andrew. "My business manager?"

"Sure, your business manager. If it wasn't for me, you'd never have taken that class and gotten the job and gotten the raise. I'm basically your agent."

"Weren't you the one trying to talk me into *not* taking the class with Mr. Sharp?"

"Reverse psychology," said Kevin as he scraped the last bit of chocolate sauce and crumbled pecans out of his now empty cup. "It was all a mind game."

"And just what is my business manager entitled to?" Andrew asked.

"Oh, I should think a decent percentage of your earnings would do," said Kevin, leaning back in his chair. "At least half."

"Here's a better idea," said Andrew, getting up to throw away his cup. "How about we both get back before we both end up losing our jobs?"

"You drive a hard bargain," said Kevin. "But, fair enough."

Later that evening, as he was getting into his bed, Andrew thought back over the conversation with Bob and Christy Roe. The entire encounter now felt surreal and, as he closed his eyes, he felt sure that he would wake up realizing it was all a dream.

CHAPTER ELEVEN
WIN-WIN INVESTING

Andrew deliberately arrived at room 205 ten minutes early so he could be waiting when Mr. Sharp arrived.

"Andrew! Surprised to see you early. Must be eager to have your brain fried with another lesson on investing?"

"Actually, I have something to show you," he said, reaching into his backpack. He pulled out his goal chart and handed it to Mr. Sharp. Over the section that said "earn a one-dollar raise at work" was a giant check mark.

"Andrew, this is awesome!" said Mr. Sharp. "You got the raise!"

"Not only that," said Andrew. "It gets even better."

Andrew relayed the whole encounter to Mr. Sharp and explained in detail the two options he had been given. When he was done talking, Mr. Sharp was quiet for a few moments. Finally, he spoke.

"I'm proud of you, Andrew," he said. "I'm also proud of the owners of The Twist. It takes a lot of foresight on their part to understand how best to motivate such a valuable employee. What are you thinking about doing?"

"I talked to my parents about it, and they're not telling me their opinions. They're saying I should choose after I consider both options carefully."

"Interesting," said Mr. Sharp. "I hope you're not disappointed that I won't be offering my opinion either."

"I had a feeling you wouldn't," said Andrew. "Could you at least give me your thoughts on each option?"

"Well let's do a cost-benefit analysis," said Mr. Sharp. He drew a line down the center of the whiteboard and on one side, he wrote "pay raise" and on the other, "profit share." "Why don't you tell me what you are thinking?" he said.

"Obviously the pay raise is a lot higher than I was hoping for and what I like about it is it is guaranteed. If I increase my hours, the pay raise is there, and if sales are down, the pay raise is there. It is safe. But it is also limited."

Mr. Sharp paused in his writing and turned to Andrew.

"Explain what you mean by that," he said.

"Well, no matter how well I do or how well the business does, I get paid the same. There's no extra incentive or anything."

"And how about the profit share?"

"The obvious benefit is that it can go up with no limit, and it motivates me to help the business increase sales. I mean if we did $10,000 more in one month, I'd make $500, and that's awesome. But there is also no guarantee. If we don't do better, then I'm stuck with my twelve dollars an hour. I just don't know—they both have strong pros and strong cons."

"If anything," said Mr. Sharp, "that should be an encouragement to you. No matter what you choose, you win. If you choose the raise, you get a three dollar an hour raise—something you probably never even anticipated as an option. If you choose the profit share, you get motivation and bonuses. Your choice isn't between something good and something bad—it's between good and good. You win either way."

"You're right," Andrew said. "I'll think about it a little more before I decide for sure."

"As you should," said Mr. Sharp. "In the meantime, let's pick up where we left off with investments. Do you remember what we ended with last class?"

"The stock market. The S&P 500 and bonds."

"Perfect," said Mr. Sharp. "Let's back up a little bit first. Tell me what you believe to be the definition of *investment*."

"Investment," said Andrew. "Investment is where you put money into something to get, hopefully, more money. Like it is a way to make your money bigger."

"You're not wrong," said Mr. Sharp, "but I want you to think in a larger context. An investment can be in anything. You can invest in finances, you can invest in education, you can invest in relationships. An investment is something where you feel your sacrifice—of money or time—will be worth it in the end. That it will generate a return on investment, or what is known as 'ROI.'"

"Like Bob and Christy Roe—they said they were investing in me."

"And they are—they believe you to be a valuable asset, and they believe that if they invest in you, it will pay off for them."

"So, investments are selfish, basically," said Andrew.

"Why do you say that?" asked Mr. Sharp.

"Well, people invest to get something for themselves. The Roes want the business to be successful because it benefits them, so they are investing in me because they want to make more money. It benefits them."

"Does it benefit anyone else?" asked Mr. Sharp.

"Well, me, I guess," said Andrew. "And anyone else who works there. We all benefit in some way."

"Have you ever heard of the phrase *win-win*?" asked Mr. Sharp.

"Sure," said Andrew. "It's like if everyone wins, then no one loses."

"You remember that *The 7 Habits of Highly Effective People* book I keep talking about? One of the habits he discusses is approaching interactions in life with a 'win-win mindset.' He explains that most people think of everyday life encounters as win-lose and think that for them to win, someone must lose. But this simply isn't true—it stems from the notion that there is only a limited amount of pie to go around, so to speak. Covey points out that the pie is not limited—there is more than enough to go around. The Roes are investing in you because it is a 'win-win'—if the business does well, you benefit, and they also benefit.

"If you think of investing in the 'win-win mindset,'" said Mr. Sharp, "then you begin to see the larger picture. When you make an investment, you are not trying to win at the expense of someone else losing. Consider an investment in a company. You are essentially giving that company some of your money hoping that the company experiences success. If the company experiences success, they win, and because they win, you also win."

"I thought you said to not invest in individual companies," said Andrew.

"You're discovering that my advice is full of paradoxes," said Mr. Sharp. "I certainly don't recommend investing in individual companies as it is riskier. However, there are times when I would encourage it. If there is a company, for instance, that you believe in wholeheartedly and you feel aligned with their larger purpose, then there is nothing wrong with investing in them because you believe the company to be on the right track. Many people choose companies just because they think the stock price will go up and yes, sometimes it does. But the bigger win is to choose a company that you firmly believe in—a company you can get behind."

"You're saying if I really like Nike and only wear Nike shoes, I should invest in the company?"

"It's more than just liking a company. It goes back to the

Why. If you believe in a company's Why, then it would be perfectly acceptable to invest in that company. Not with everything, of course, but with part of your portfolio."

"What if I don't like a company? Is that when you would 'short' it?" Andrew asked.

"Where did you hear about shorting a company?" Mr. Sharp asked.

"From a movie I watched. *The Big Short.* The one where those guys bet against the stock market and won."

"I do like that movie," said Mr. Sharp. "Let me ask you— were those guys who won the bet in that movie considered heroes?"

"I guess so," said Andrew. "I mean the movie focused on them the whole time."

"It's an interesting question," said Mr. Sharp. "They shorted mortgages and they won a lot of money. But because they won, millions of people lost. People lost their jobs, their homes, their retirement plans, everything. Their win was really a win-lose."

"What is a short, then?"

"In basic terms, it is a bet *against* a company or fund. While the purchase of stock in a company is a vote of confidence that the company will grow and prosper, a short is betting that the company's share price will drop or that they will even go bankrupt. The movie focused on the Great Recession of 2008 and what is called the 'subprime mortgage crisis.' The characters in the movie realized that banks had been issuing dicey mortgage loans for homes and they realized that soon, the collections of mortgages sold as 'mortgage bonds' would crumble. That's the nature of a short—seeing a problem no one else sees and betting against the company or entity. Either way, the win, if it happens, comes with some sort of loss. While shorts can certainly make a person a lot of money, they do come with a lot of risk."

"So do you not recommend them?"

"Personally, no," said Mr. Sharp. "Ultimately, everyone has to make up his or her own mind when it comes to investing but, for me, I prefer to stick to opportunities where I win because someone else also wins. Does that make sense?"

"I think so," said Andrew.

"Let me show you something else when it comes to investing. Like we said earlier, investing is more than just the stock market—it is about securing an asset. Have you ever studied the difference between an asset and a liability?" asked Mr. Sharp.

Andrew shook his head.

"Excellent," said Mr. Sharp. "In basic economic terms, an asset is something you own that has value while a liability is something that costs you."

"Like student loan debt," said Andrew.

"Exactly—student loan debt is a liability, but the degree you earn is an asset."

Mr. Sharp opened his bag and pulled out a purple book with the title *Rich Dad, Poor Dad* on the front.

"Robert Kiyosaki, the author of this book, goes a little further with his definitions of assets and liabilities. He explains that an asset is not just something of value that you own, but something that generates revenue for you. In other words, if you own a fancy suit that you paid $500 for, Kiyosaki would say that it is not an asset because, even though it has value to you, it does not generate revenue.

"It is a radical definition," continued Mr. Sharp, "because it flies in the face of the traditional belief that if you owned it, it was an asset. Like a car, for example. If you own your car and it is worth $20,000, then traditionally a person's net worth would include that $20,000 car. Kiyosaki says that is not true—the car does not generate revenue. In fact, it does the opposite. Cars are expensive; they require insurance and regular maintenance, not to mention gas."

"Trust me, I know that firsthand—my dad is going over all those expenses with me now that I have my license. It's going to be a lot more money than I thought. For now, I'm borrowing his car but I'm paying for my own gas and insurance."

"Welcome to the wonderful world of growing up," said Mr. Sharp. "Assets and liabilities. A car may seem like an asset, especially when you don't have one, but soon it is clear that it is in the liability category. Remember that if it does not generate revenue, according to Kiyosaki, it cannot be an asset. An asset, by that definition, would be an investment in an index fund like the S&P 500. That investment generates revenue, upward of 10 or 12 percent a year, so it is earning you money without you having to do anything else. Another example would be a book. If you write a book and publish it, it will earn you money as long as people continue to buy it, so that 'intellectual property' would be considered an asset."

"That's what you want to do," Andrew said, smiling.

"Indeed it is," said Mr. Sharp. "And I'm pleased to say that since our conversation, I've already written the first three chapters."

"That's awesome," said Andrew.

"Well, it's a start," said Mr. Sharp. "Can you think of anything else that would qualify as an asset?"

"Earlier you said that while student loans were liabilities, the degree was an asset."

"Yes," said Mr. Sharp. "Can you explain how?"

"I think because with a degree you can get a good job and so it generates revenue because it helps you get more money because of your education."

"Bingo," said Mr. Sharp. "Now speaking of student loans, Kiyosaki explains that while assets generate revenue, liabilities suck up that revenue. He argues that the key to financial intelligence is shrewdly determining the difference between assets and liabilities and then investing in assets. For instance, let's say you had $30,000. You could buy a nice car, or you could buy stock in the S&P 500. Most people are inclined to buy the car because they need to get around and they spend so much time in their cars. But consider that most cars depreciate at a rate of 20 percent a year for the first few years.

"That means that one year after buying the car, it is now worth $24,000. It cost you, effectively, $6,000. Definition of a liability. Now imagine if you bought a used car for $10,000. After the first year it, drops 20 percent and you lose $2,000. Quite a bit less than $6,000. And with the remaining $20,000, you could invest in the stock market and earn $2,400 or so, which would not only offset your loss on the car but keep you from going in the red. That's the point— make smarter decisions with how you spend your money so you can invest more in assets and less in liabilities."

"Basically, you want your assets to be more than your liabilities," said Andrew.

"Yes—that's the concept behind net worth," said Mr. Sharp. "Simply put, your net worth is a compilation of all of your assets added up and then all of your liabilities subtracted. That's why many people, right out of college, have a negative net worth—they have virtually no assets, but they have lots of debt. The goal is to get out of all debt and build up assets that continue to generate revenues so that it adds to your net worth."

"How about a house; is that an asset?"

"This is actually where I disagree with Kiyosaki," said Mr. Sharp. "He argues that a house is not an asset but is actually a liability because it does not generate revenue, and it costs so much to keep up. While he has a valid argument, I believe that having a house has benefits that outweigh the costs. Did you know, for instance, that houses increase in value at about 4 percent a year?"

"Four percent?" asked Andrew. "That's not a lot."

"From an outside perspective, no, it is not," said Mr. Sharp. "Certainly a lot less than you would make in other investments. But consider that most people only put a down payment on their home to begin. Here's what I mean."

Mr. Sharp returned to the whiteboard and, with his characteristic enthusiasm, began to write while he continued talking.

"The first thing to keep in mind is that you should wait until you are settled before buying a house. I'm not saying you must be married with three kids and a dog kind of settled, but you should have an established career and not have the possibility of job change looming on the horizon. The last thing you want is to purchase a house and then have to move right away and not have time to build what's called 'equity.' The easiest way to think of equity is to consider how much you owe on your mortgage subtracted from the overall value of the home. If you owe $200,000 and your home is worth $250,000, then you have $50,000 in equity. This is why you want to make sure you are buying your house in an area that will go up in value. There's a whole science to it, but the easiest tip is to look for a house in a neighborhood with good schools. You don't want the most expensive house on the street, and you don't want to buy more house than you can afford.

"But let's focus on the numbers," said Mr. Sharp, continuing. "Here are some starting assumptions: You decide to purchase a home in your mid-twenties. You pick one that is on the market for $200,000. You make a down payment of 5 percent or $10,000 and finance the rest with a mortgage loan. You still with me?"

Andrew nodded but looked uncertain.

"A down payment is what you pay the bank before they agree to give you the rest of the money to pay the purchase price—in the form of a mortgage loan that will require monthly payments. People used to say you had to put 20 percent down on your house and while that's a great goal, it is often unattainable for your first house. Twenty percent down on a $200,000 house is $40,000 and that's a big amount to save up. A down payment of $10,000 is far more realistic. You take that $10,000 and go to the bank or mortgage broker and ask for a mortgage to pay for the house. They give you the remaining $190,000 and charge you interest on the loan. Right now, most of these mortgage rates are hovering around 4 percent interest and that is calculated annually and then paid as part of the monthly mortgage payments. That means that if you borrow $190,000 at 4 percent, then every year, you pay $7,600 in interest payments on top of your principal payments. Principal payments are payments toward the actual loan."

"So close to $8,000 is just giving away money to the bank. Sounds like a lose-win," said Andrew. "The banks come away with a huge win while I lose."

"It sounds that way, but it is actually a win-win, as long as you get a good interest rate and a fair mortgage. Most mortgages are thirty-year loans, but they also offer other options like fifteen-year loans. I'm a huge fan of the fifteen-year mortgages because, even though your payment is higher, you can often get lower interest rates. Not only will you pay off your home in half the time, but also you'll most likely pay significantly less interest. Check these numbers out," Mr. Sharp said as he pulled up an online mortgage calculator and displayed it on the projector. "If you get a $190,000 loan for thirty years at a 4 percent rate and you take thirty years to pay it off, you end up paying $326,552 for the loan."

"What?" said Andrew in disbelief, "That's crazy! That's $126,000 more than the original amount of the loan!"

"I know—and it is definitely not a win-win arrangement. But, if you get the same loan amount for fifteen years and still at 4 percent, even though you'd probably get an even better rate, you end up paying $252,973 by the end."

"That's almost $75,000 less! Why wouldn't you do that?" asked Andrew.

"A good question," said Mr. Sharp. "Usually because you just don't know. As I've said countless times, schools don't teach this stuff, so people just don't know. Second, though, is because it makes your payments higher. If you did that fifteen-year loan, you are paying over $1,400 a month between your principal and interest. If you went for thirty years, you are paying just over $900. People see those numbers and they think the $900 payment is better for their budget, so they go for thirty years. They are ignoring the big picture and settling for the short-term benefit of more money each month. It's sad, but it is definitely the more popular option."

"It's stupid," said Andrew. "You're wasting $75,000 and an extra fifteen years."

"I don't disagree," said Mr. Sharp. "But let's return to the notion of a liability versus an asset." He began erasing a section of the whiteboard to make room for new calculations. "If you can follow my train of thought, you'll see something super cool.

"Let's say you invest $10,000 into a house that is worth $200,000," continued Mr. Sharp. "Each year, that home increases in value by about 4 percent, as I mentioned earlier, because that is the average at which home values increase. Assuming, of course, that your home is in a good area that is experiencing growth. That's a discussion for another day, though. If your home is increasing by 4 percent each year, then after owning it for five years, it is worth $243,000. Pretty nice, huh?"

"Yeah, sounds like a good investment," Andrew said.

"Now remember that you purchased this home for a $10,000 down payment. That means that in terms of an asset, you own $10,000 in the house. In five years, however, the house is worth $43,000 more, which means that your

$10,000 turned into $53,000 in just five years. That's about a 45 percent return on your money, which is better than you will ever see in your other accounts."

Andrew's eyes were wide from following the array of numbers Mr. Sharp was writing all over the whiteboard.

"Now, all along," said Mr. Sharp, "you had to make your mortgage payment along with your homeowner's insurance, property taxes, and regular bills associated with homeownership. But in the end, the price will be about the same as renting and yet you are also paying off your mortgage. Each month as you make that $1,400 house payment (which includes the interest on your loan and money toward the mortgage), about $800 of it will be going toward your mortgage. That means that after the five years are up, you'll owe about $137,000 instead of $190,000. That puts your total asset in the home at $106,000. In just five years, you went from $10,000 to over $100,000. *BOOM!*" Mr. Sharp dropped his whiteboard marker with a definitive gesture. "That's the power of investing. That's what gets me excited. Questions?"

"I just, well, wow. I don't really know what to say."

"Think of it like this—your home, if picked carefully and mortgaged properly, can be perhaps your strongest asset. It's a great system, but it does have its downsides. For instance, that money doesn't really exist until you move and once you move, you must pay realtor fees and inspection fees and other items, but you still make a great deal of money if you bought a house in a good area with rising property values. After five years, you can sell and move to a bigger house and put 20 percent down. That's how people move up in houses through investing. And as you move up, your home generates even more revenue because 4 percent on a $300,000 home is $12,000 a year. That's your money making money. That's the definition of an asset."

"Is putting your money toward a house down payment even better than putting it in the stock market?" said Andrew.

"That's where you have to decide for yourself," said Mr. Sharp. "So much about owning a home is wrapped up in the emotional experience of having a place to call your own, which may not be a factor for everyone. Both pursuits have value and, in my case, I feel it is worth investing in both. But since you ask that question, let me show you a really cool thing you can do with your investments. We talked earlier about Roth IRAs—remember?"

"Yes," said Andrew, "the retirement accounts that grow tax-free."

"Excellent," said Mr. Sharp. "I told you that you couldn't touch the earnings until you turn fifty-nine and a half. That wasn't entirely true."

"It's not?"

"There are exceptions," said Mr. Sharp. "One of these exceptions is the first-time home buyer exception. If you are a first-time home buyer, the government will let you take up to $10,000 from your IRA to fund the down payment on your house. They see you buying a home as a good thing for the economy, so they want to encourage you to do it. This means that you can withdraw the money that has grown tax-free and use it to fuel one of the great investments of your life—your home. This is why it is so important to begin funding that Roth IRA as early as possible—the quicker it grows, the quicker you can withdraw some to start bigger investments."

"But I thought the point of the Roth IRA was to keep the money in there to create the retirement account. If I take the money out, won't I just be starting over?"

"It's another situation where you have to do a cost-benefit analysis. Does the benefit of fueling the asset of a home outweigh the cost of depleting your IRA? It's a hard decision, but the decision is made easier if you start fueling that IRA as soon as possible so the withdrawal won't hurt as much. If you start your plan now with the $250 a month you mentioned, you'd have over $52,000 in there by the time you turn twenty-six. Taking $10,000 of that out for your down payment doesn't look that bad at that point."

"True," said Andrew, "I guess not."

"Tell you what," Mr. Sharp said when he saw Andrew blink a few times, "that was a lot for today. Let's stop there for now and pick up next class with more about investing. Here's an assignment for you—talk with your parents about their mortgage. Ask them how much they put down when they bought your house and then look up the current price online. The website Zillow does a pretty good job of estimating home values. See if you can determine how much money their money has made since moving into the house."

CHAPTER TWELVE
MARKET CYCLES

"Your semester is almost over—how are things wrapping up?"

Andrew's father had just entered the office where Andrew was perched in front of the computer entering numbers into an online calculator.

"Good," he said.

"Good, huh?" said his father. "How about a little more info than that. How's the class with Mr. Sharp?"

"That's what I'm working on," said Andrew. "Now he's got me looking into buying a house."

"Buying a house?" his father asked. "That seems a bit extreme, even for him."

"Not buying one now, obviously," said Andrew. "He wants me to start looking into how homes can build equity and add to net worth."

"Interesting. He's correct in that getting a house can be a great investment, if it is the right time in your life and if you choose the right house. A lot can go wrong, however, if it is the wrong time or the wrong house. There's a reason your mother and I waited so long before purchasing a home."

"Mr. Sharp is saying I should buy one in my twenties."

"Really? Wow, that's ambitious. Not crazy, of course, just ambitious. What's his reasoning?"

Andrew went over, in-depth, his previous class and explained all the logic behind the home's increasing value along with pointers on assets and liabilities. By the time he was finished, his father was looking at him with a sense of awe and respect.

"Andrew," his father said, "you've learned more in just a few months than I learned in twenty years. And most of my learning came from mistakes. All in all, I'd say this class has probably been the most helpful one you've taken yet in high school. Maybe even in all of your schooling."

"It's pretty crazy stuff," said Andrew. "Definitely worth it."

"And work? How's that going these days?"

"I love it—did I tell you that they finalized a budget for me? When I told them that I would go with the profit share choice rather than the hourly raise, they, Bob and Christy, told me that I have $200 a month to try out some advertising ideas."

"That's great, Andrew," said his father. "What sort of things are you going to try?"

"I don't know yet. Actually, I was hoping to ask you and Mom."

"Well, we'd love to help. This certainly has been an exciting year so far for you. For all of us, I suppose."

Andrew finished up his spreadsheet and turned off his computer before heading down to dinner. After dinner, he sat around the table with his parents and brainstormed for at least an hour about how to drive more business to The Twist. Before they were finished, they had over a dozen ideas and Andrew felt more ready than ever to try them out.

His excitement carried into his next class with Mr. Sharp that following Tuesday. When he arrived in the classroom, he found the whiteboard mostly covered with two large pictures: one was of a bear standing on two legs growling, while the other was of a large bull in an attack stance.

"Welcome, Andrew," said Mr. Sharp. "I thought as we start to wrap up this class, we should cover a few basics."

"Hmm," said Andrew, "Basics, huh? Are you going to lecture me about checking accounts again?"

"Well, perhaps not that basic," said Mr. Sharp, smiling. "Perhaps I should revise my opening statement to say 'fundamentals.' Today we are going to cover some fundamentals about the stock market."

"I assume that's what the bear and the bull pictures are for?"

"Yes—we'll be using those pictures in our discussion. Any idea why?"

"I've heard about the bull," Andrew said, "Isn't there one in New York or something?"

"That's 'Charging Bull,'" said Mr. Sharp, as he pointed to the picture on the whiteboard. "Isn't he a cutie?"

"Uh, not quite," said Andrew.

"Charging Bull is a bronze statue in the financial district of Manhattan in New York City. He's a sort of symbol of a cycle in the stock market."

"And the bear?"

"Another symbol of a cycle. Not quite as much fun, as I'll explain. To begin, there are four primary cycles you need to be aware of when it comes to the stock market. I'm going to cover each of them but understand, from the start, that the point of today's lesson is that the market is full of ups and downs. It may be on a tear one day, going higher and higher, and then the next day, it shoots down below the start of the previous day. Up, and down, up and down. Sometimes down, down, and down. Somethings up, up, and up. It is an ongoing cycle of the market, and it can wreak havoc on the short-term investor because of all the uncertainty. Up to this point in the class, I've been presenting a mostly optimistic view of investments, but today we're going to get into what happens when things take a turn for the worse."

"So, you're saying it's not all sunshine and rainbows when it comes to investing your money?"

"Far from it," said Mr. Sharp. "Long-term investors require a strong stomach because they will go through periods where they lose money. It's important to understand the market cycles so you can roughly know what to expect and brace yourself for losses."

Mr. Sharp drew a flat arrow on the board and wrote the number one next to it.

"The first cycle is the bottom, or the falling out. This is where things have reached their low point and the market is just plain down. Not necessarily a complete crash, but in general, stocks have tanked, and it is not a good time for short-term investors who just lost a bunch of money."

"So should you get out of your investments when that happens?" asked Andrew.

"That depends," said Mr. Sharp, "on your personal stance regarding investments. The problem is that many people do try to get out and, in doing so, they lose a lot of their money. They also lose the chance to gain some or all of that money back when the cycle changes. The tricky thing is timing the cycle—it is hard to say when the true bottom has hit. Things could always get worse and yet they could always get better. Trying to time things is nothing short of gambling."

Mr. Sharp returned to the board and, next to the flat arrow, drew an arrow curving upward.

"The second cycle," continued Mr. Sharp, "is where it gets fun. Enter our friend, Charging Bull. The bull market is a growth market, one that is full of optimism and high expectations. Everyone gets excited during bull markets as numbers just keep going up. This is where we get terms like *bullish*, which means optimistic about growth."

"But why is it called a bull market?" asked Andrew.

"Think of the primary feature on the bull that gives it its persona. What is the attribute we associate with bulls?"

"Charging," said Andrew.

"Yes, they charge," said Mr. Sharp, "But what do they lead with when they charge?"

"Horns," Andrew said.

"Exactly. When a bull rears its head, its horns go up in the air. That going up motion is associated with stock market growth. Individual stocks go up, indices go up, and often the entire market goes up. During a bull market, people are racing to buy in and ride the market as high as it will go. Again, though, is the timing issue."

"We don't know when it will end," said Andrew.

"Precisely—it is hard to say how long the bull market will last. Could it last a month, three months, even a year? Several years? Absolutely. But it can also change tomorrow. When it does change, it usually brings about our third cycle, the plateau."

Mr. Sharp drew a straight, flat line after the curve of the second cycle.

"The plateau is where the growth stops and the market levels out. Nothing super special here, but prices remain steady, and things aren't really moving one way or another. Kind of boring. But, for some investors, that can be a good thing as it means less volatility and crazy changes."

"I assume this leads to the fourth cycle, which is a downward curve?"

"As I've said before, you're a fast learner. Yes, the final cycle is the slide back down, which is often called a correction. Enter our friend, the bear. Have you ever seen a bear attack on YouTube or anything?"

"I saw a pretty gruesome one in the movie *The Revenant*," Andrew said.

"Agreed—super gruesome. Probably not the best example for what I wanted to say because that bear flat out charged Leonardo DiCaprio, but often bears attack by swiping down with their powerful paws. That downward motion is where this cycle of the market gets its name. The bear market swipes us downward until we bottom out to repeat cycle one again. It's more or less the opposite of the bull market—that's why the terms *bull* and *bear* are used so often when it comes to the stock market. When it is a bull market, people are generally buying, and when it is a bear market, people are generally selling."

"But you're saying you should stay in regardless?" asked Andrew.

"Again, it depends. A bear market can be a great market for certain investments, like bonds, which, because of their relative safety, people flock to when things look uncertain. An investment in bonds might go up during the market downturn, while an investment in stocks will usually go down. This is why I favor a diversity of investments so that you can create a sort of hedge, or protection, around your money. The more you diversify, the more you create a safety net. It means you won't earn as much as possible during the bull market, but conversely, it means you won't lose as much as possible during the bear market. It has to do with understanding risk."

Here Mr. Sharp paused and wrote "unsystematic" and "systematic" on the whiteboard.

"Here's a crash course in understanding risk," he said, pointing to the words. "First up is unsystematic risk. This is the risk that comes from an individual stock or sector. For instance, if all of your money were in Apple, you would be far from diversified. You might have a great few months or even years, but if something happened to the technology industry and Apple got hit hard, you would be in bad shape with your investment. Let's say that a report came out that iPhones were linked to a certain cancer and Apple's stock dipped 20 percent overnight. If your whole portfolio is Apple, you'd lose 20 percent of everything—that's unsystematic risk."

"If I own more stock than just Apple though, then I can avoid unsystematic risk? Basically, if I diversify, I limit my risk?"

"Exactly," said Mr. Sharp. "Unsystematic risk is risk you can wipe out by broadening your investment approach. Think larger than single stocks and single industries. That's why the S&P 500, which is often used as a benchmark for stock market performance, is a great investment because—"

"Because it is owning a piece of all five hundred companies," said Andrew. "I'm getting the hang of this."

"I can see that," said Mr. Sharp. "That leaves us with systematic risk—this is the risk that can't be mitigated or diversified away. This is the risk that comes with events outside of our control. If the government announced that it is going to war with a particular country, or if oil prices skyrocket, or if a natural resource dries up, the stock market would be affected, and because you can't do anything about this, it's called systematic risk. The goal of the savvy investor is to get rid of as much unsystematic risk as possible and learn to accept systematic risk."

"Basically, you're saying that the market is always going up and down and up and down?" asked Andrew.

"More or less," said Mr. Sharp. "Let's just say it is far from steady. And there's no definitive length of time for each cycle. Sometimes the bear market can last an incredibly long time and the market takes months or even years to return to a high point. Other times, after a correction, it can bounce right back up. There are a lot of unknowns, which can certainly complicate things for investors. And don't assume that the cycles have to work in the same order—you might go from a bull market to a plateau back to a bull market. Again, uncertainty is the only thing that is certain."

"But if I'm in it for the long term, it doesn't matter as much, right?"

"Not in the long term," said Mr. Sharp, "but it can be a hard one to remain steadfast, especially as you are watching the value of your portfolio drop day after day. If the market crashes, you see all your hard-earned money slip away, often at a rate much faster than it accumulated, and that is enough for anyone to lose their cool and give in to the urge to sell and mitigate losses. After all, losing money is losing money no matter how you look at it."

"Just to clarify," said Andrew, "are you saying just stay in through the bad cycles?"

"I'm saying prepare yourself for the bad times because, like it or not, they will come. You will lose money and the market will crash and things will go poorly. And not just with your investments, but in your life as well. You will have an emergency where you need to pull some or all of your money from savings. You will encounter an unexpected change that requires you to move or change jobs or pivot in some crucial way. These are unavoidable aspects of life and the best we can do is hope for the best but always, and I mean *always*, prepare for the worst."

"You weren't kidding when you said some of this would be discouraging," said Andrew. "One class you're telling me I'll be a millionaire, and now you're telling me I'll be losing all my money and living on the street."

"Perhaps not to that extreme," said Mr. Sharp, "but consider how much worse it would be if you weren't prepared for the inevitable tragedy. If you lose your job and have six months of savings in the bank, that tragedy is far better than losing your job and being completely broke. I'm saying be prepared for the tragedy and, keep in mind, when one bad thing happens, others are not far behind. That's why preparation and financial security are key."

"It kind of feels like it might be safer to just bury my money in the backyard, so I don't have to worry about losing it when the market crashes."

"Ha," said Mr. Sharp, "you're not alone in that sentiment. Unfortunately, those who take that approach miss out on all the wonderful parts of investing. When it comes to the stock market, here's what we know from history: The market always goes back up. Always. It may take a few weeks or months or even years, but it does go back up and often quite higher than when the correction happened in the first place. If you can stomach the ups and downs of systematic risk, you'll come out ahead in the end. That's why I say an 'average' of 10 percent over the years. Some years you'll lose money, pure and simple. Other years, you'll have a terrific return. But if you stay the course, year after year, you'll settle into a comfortable return overall. If you bury your money in the ground, it will not only stay the same amount, but it will actually decrease."

"Decrease?" asked Andrew. "What do you mean? Is a squirrel going to eat it or something?"

"Well, that's certainly a possibility," said Mr. Sharp, "But what I'm referring to is inflation. Have you ever heard your parents or some other adult talk about how things used to be a lot less expensive when they were kids?"

"Sure," said Andrew, "my dad does that all the time. He

says candy bars used to be a quarter and now some of them are over a dollar."

"That's inflation at work," said Mr. Sharp. "I'm not going to go into it in complete depth, but the important thing to understand is that over time, the value of money inherently decreases. One thousand dollars today will buy more than $1,000 ten years from now. On average, inflation increases at a rate of around 3 percent per year. And it's compounded, which means that it works the same way as our calculations for compound interest."

Mr. Sharp pulled a calculator from his bag and began pressing numbers in quick succession.

"Here's what I mean," he said, turning to write on the board. "Something that costs $1,000 today will, in ten years, cost $1,343. In twenty years, it will cost $1,806. Each year, with inflation, the value of money drops, so, as an investor, you need to stay ahead of the curve and be sure that your money is earning more than the rate of inflation. If you bury your money in the backyard, you are basically letting it wither away at the rate of 3 percent a year."

"So, you're saying that 3 percent of all my returns each year is just keeping up with inflation?"

"Keep in mind that in an ideal scenario, everything is increasing by 3 percent on average a year, and that includes your paycheck. It's not a perfect system, but it's considered the cost-of-living increase—a salary that is $30,000 today will be closer to $131,500 by the time you are sixty-five. It's just the nature of how the financial system works. It's also why getting at least a 10 percent return, on average, is so important so that you can stay well above the rate of inflation and plan for your future."

"I don't know," said Andrew, "it all just sounds pretty confusing."

"It can seem that way," said Mr. Sharp, "but the important thing to keep in mind is that the informed investor is the smart investor. You already know far more about how money works when invested than most people twice your age, and your financial knowledge does not have to stop at this class. I'd recommend that you continue your financial education far beyond this semester and well into the rest of your life. Take the time to read a few articles every week, listen to some of the audiobooks I've recommended, seek out other classes or seminars on the topic. Just keep going because the more you learn, the more you will understand how to bring about financial freedom. Remember the seed tree metaphor we talked about during the compound interest lesson. It applies to more than just money—while just a few trees can repopulate the whole field, just a few articles or audiobooks can spread wisdom throughout your life and change the trajectory of your future for the better."

Andrew nodded to signify his understanding.

"In closing," said Mr. Sharp, "if you take nothing else out of this class, then take this—don't live your life in bondage to your money. Debt is nothing more than imprisonment and true freedom lies in mastering money before it masters you."

"You're getting pretty inspirational, Mr. Sharp," said Andrew, smiling. "I kind of feel like you should have some background music playing or something."

"Not a bad idea," said Mr. Sharp. "Now get out of here before I find another soapbox where I can wax eloquent."

CHAPTER THIRTEEN
LIFE LESSONS

Each December, the school hosted an annual college fair. From around the country, over fifty colleges and universities set up booths in the massive school gymnasium to advertise their campuses and their programs. Students from surrounding schools as well as homeschool students attended to walk around and learn what these institutions had to offer. The event was held on a Thursday evening and, at the special urging of his parents, Andrew had requested time off work to attend.

"Dude, check it out," Kevin said, holding up a coffee mug emblazoned with "Harvard University" and "Veritas."

"Cool," Andrew said. "I imagine that's where you're planning on going?"

"Ha, I wish," said Kevin. "But at least I can pretend with this mug. There is so much free stuff they're giving out tonight—I should have brought a bigger bag. Hey, hold this for me for a minute." Kevin thrust the mug into Andrew's hand and raced off to grab a tote bag at the Northern Kentucky University table.

"Ah, headed for the Ivy League I see."

Andrew turned around to face none other than Mr. Sharp.

"What are you doing here?" he asked.

"A little birdie told me this was a hopping event at the school," said Mr. Sharp. "Figured I couldn't miss it."

"Hey!" said Kevin, racing back and holding a bag already half full of college paraphernalia. "This is perfect—now I can get even more stuff."

"Kevin, this is Mr. Sharp, my finance teacher."

"Hi," said Kevin. "I chose Art of War instead of your class."

"So I heard," said Mr. Sharp. "I trust it is a good class?"

"It's fine," Kevin said. "At least there's no homework or anything."

"Well, I'd be more than happy to have you in a future class," said Mr. Sharp.

"All right," said Kevin. "Hey, Andrew, want to go check out those free water bottles at the Duke table?"

"Coming," said Andrew, turning to Mr. Sharp. "It was good seeing you here, but I—"

"Go," said Mr. Sharp. "No worries—join your friend and enjoy the free stuff. I'll see you in class next week. Our last one at that."

"Crazy," said Andrew. "The semester is basically over. OK, see you!"

Andrew caught up to Kevin as he was shoving a handful

of pens in his pocket before moving on to the stress balls at the Purdue table.

"I'm going to miss that class," Andrew said, looking back at Mr. Sharp, who was now engaged in conversation with Mr. Lantz.

"What, with Mr. Scissors? Dude seems pretty boring."

"No," Andrew said, "his class is really interesting. You should have taken it with me."

"And missed watching the entire series of *Band of Brothers*? Ha, no thanks."

Andrew and Kevin continued making their way around the booths until both were unable to carry anything else. Driving home that night in his father's car, Andrew thought about the fact that he only had one class left with Mr. Sharp. He felt far more knowledgeable about finance and investing, but he also felt that there was still so much left to understand. His mind soon turned to other things, though, and by the time he was pulling in his driveway, the whole evening felt like a distant memory.

"Well, here we go," said Mr. Sharp as Andrew entered room 205 that following week. "All good things come to an end. I thought we could end our class by addressing your questions. You can ask me anything, and I'll answer as best as I can."

"So, anything?"

"Sure, anything we covered or didn't cover or that you want to know. Can be personal, finance-related, business, anything."

"OK," said Andrew, setting down his books. "In that case, where did you go to college?"

"College, huh? I'm assuming your question has nothing to do with the college fair last week?" Mr. Sharp said, smiling, "I actually went to a local school—Cincinnati State. I studied business, took extra classes, and graduated one semester early."

"I guess I thought maybe you went to a big, flashy school or something."

"Flashy like that mug Kevin handed you? Good ol' Harvard? I thought about it. I wanted to, to an extent. Do you remember, early on in class, when I mentioned that someone mentored me when I was your age?"

"Yes," said Andrew.

"That someone was an uncle of mine. Uncle Mark. He taught me a lot of things about finance and business and life. The most important thing, however, was about debt. You see, Uncle Mark lived his life under the shadow of debt until he was forty years old. He had student loan debt, car debt, credit card debt; you name it. When he finally got everything paid off, he resolved to help other people avoid debt at all costs. I guess you could say he took me under his wing and made me promise to stay away from debt."

"Is that why you went to a local college?"

"It is. I had applications in at all sorts of schools—especially schools in California. I truly envisioned myself in LA or San Diego or even Long Beach. I also applied to New York University and even Princeton."

"Wow—Princeton?"

"I said I applied—not that I got in," said Mr. Sharp, smiling. "I ended up getting accepted at a few of these schools but after scholarships and financial aid, most of them would have ended up being around $30,000 a year."

"It's probably even higher now," said Andrew.

"Undoubtedly," said Mr. Sharp. "Last I heard, Princeton was close to $75,000 before scholarships and aid. And that's per year. Even if it gets knocked down to $40,000, that's still $160,000 for four years."

"That's a lot," said Andrew.

"And it's not just the Ivy League schools," said Mr. Sharp. "Here in Ohio, if you go to a private school like Denison, you're looking at a minimum of $50,000 in tuition alone. After a while, you just have to ask yourself if it is worth it. In the end, is the $200,000 in debt worth a degree from a school like that? In my experience, the school you attended matters less than the way you present yourself. A degree from Cincinnati State has in no way hindered me from making my way in the business world."

"Most of my friends are planning on going out of state," Andrew said. "Northwestern, Purdue, and the University of Michigan are big contenders. I haven't really even started looking into it yet, and my parents have been pretty hands-off about the process, but I didn't want to stay close to home for college."

"By no means should you," said Mr. Sharp. "For me it

was convenient because I had free room and board with my parents, but there are plenty of state schools with in-state tuition that have great programs depending on what you are interested in."

"Doesn't it look better to go to a more reputable school, though? I mean, if I went to Princeton, wouldn't I get a better job than someone who stayed local?"

"You would think," said Mr. Sharp, "but that's a bit of a misconception. I was talking to a recruiter just the other day who works for P&G. His job is to find qualified candidates at college campuses to fill key positions at the company. He said that given the choice between a grad from Stanford who was given everything on a silver platter and a grad from some no-name college who had to work hard for everything in life, he'd choose the grad from the no-name college every time. He said certain things, like work ethic and determination, can't be taught."

"Maybe so," said Andrew, "but still, a degree from a good college would be an asset, right? That's what we talked about the other day."

"An asset, yes," said Mr. Sharp. "But at what cost? Remember that assets are supposed to generate revenue and a degree from a solid college will certainly help land a good job that will bring in a consistent revenue stream. Consider, though, that degree, if it comes with a large amount of debt, may actually be better categorized as a liability. Look at this statistic."

Mr. Sharp went to his computer and began typing. He then connected the projector to display his screen on the whiteboard.

"College graduates of 2019 had an average student loan debt of $30,000 for a bachelor's degree. And this is an average—on the high end, some were over $100,000. We talked about this earlier, but that means that upon graduation, students are starting out a year's salary or more in the negative and they'll work for years to pay off that loan. Every dollar in debt is a dollar subtracted from their net worth, and that's why many people in their early to mid-twenties have a negative net worth. The key to financial freedom is staying out of debt and building wealth, like we've been talking about all along, so avoiding student loans wherever and however possible is a large part of that."

"I don't know how my parents will feel about that," Andrew said. "They aren't pushing any one college or anything, but I doubt they want me going to a local community college."

"And by no means do you have to—I'm merely saying that often the big-name colleges are touted as being a better option than they really are. It's smart to do a cost-benefit analysis before you make a college decision to make sure that the money spent is completely worth it. But enough on that, let's move on. Any other questions?"

"Um, not really, I guess. Do you have any advice that you haven't already given?"

"Advice," said Mr. Sharp. "That's something I'm full of. Probably have a bit too much to give. Yes, since you are kind enough to ask, I do have some."

Mr. Sharp turned off his computer and the projector and grabbed a dry erase marker. On the board he wrote "Life Advice."

"OK, you ready?" Mr. Sharp asked, looking at Andrew. "I'm about to unload all sorts of stuff on you. And I should note that, while most of what I talked about in this class is sound financial advice, I'm about to venture into subjective territory. Many people would disagree with me on some of these points, but I've found them to be true in my own life and firmly believe in them."

"Bring it," said Andrew, "I can take it."

"First," Mr. Sharp said, writing a large number one on the board, "is to pursue happiness."

"Are the other ones going to be 'life' and 'liberty'?" Andrew asked.

"Very funny," said Mr. Sharp. "By pursue happiness, I mean find something that brings you fulfillment and go after it. Chase it down. Don't settle for a career you are not passionate about, even if it pays more. So many students these days want to become lawyers and doctors and business executives, but they are only trying to please their parents. It doesn't have to be about the money—we saw how you can retire a multimillionaire by never making more than $50,000 or $60,000 a year."

"Don't be a lawyer," Andrew said, "I'm writing that down."

"Perhaps I should clarify," said Mr. Sharp, smiling. "There's nothing wrong with being a lawyer as long as it brings you happiness. If you enjoy being in the courtroom or researching the law, then by all means. But don't do it to please somebody else. That leads to my next one, which is 'get married.'"

"Seriously?" Andrew said.

"Seriously. It's a fact that married people are happier overall. Don't get so caught up in your studies and career that you fail to pursue a serious relationship. Find a partner you connect with on all levels. But also someone who shares your priorities and values. I'm a big fan of getting married early and not waiting until you're in your late twenties or early thirties. By then, you are set in your ways and you'll have a harder time opening up your life to someone else."

"So let me get this straight," said Andrew. "Your life advice so far is to be happy and get married young."

"Hearing your summation makes me think there may be a few gaps," said Mr. Sharp, "but you've got the basic gist. On the note of marriage, be sure to discuss your financial outlook with a prospective partner—there is not much worse than entering a marriage relationship with someone who is not on the same page as you regarding spending and saving. You should talk about budgeting, about financial goals, about spending habits, even about retirement. Financial stress has been the downfall of many a marriage, which is actually my third point: 'Don't Get Divorced.'"

"You're really taking this whole life advice thing and running with it," said Andrew.

"This one connects directly to our whole class on finance. Divorce ruins your finances, pure and simple. It can also ruin your life, but we can focus on finances here," Mr. Sharp said, smiling. "Seriously, though, when couples split up, they have to divide their assets in half, and dividing your assets in half means cutting your net worth up and halting all that great compound interest and wealth building. Often it means starting back at zero, except you have a lot less time to get those investments back up and running."

"What if you absolutely have to get divorced, like there's no other option?"

"That's why I urge people to really get to know the person they are marrying. Especially with regard to financial values. I'm not saying divorce is never an option, but I am saying that in terms of life advice, staying married is the better financial option. There's a lot more we could go into on this point, but I don't want to belabor it. Besides, I have so much more life advice to give!"

"I don't know how much more I can take," Andrew said with a smirk.

"I'm going to start summing up a few of the things we've already discussed as more life advice," said Mr. Sharp, returning to the whiteboard. "For instance, open a checking and savings account."

"Done," said Andrew.

"Get a job and set up direct deposit."

"Check."

"Create a budget and stick to it. Revise, if necessary, but be sure that what is going out is less than what is coming in."

"Good to go," said Andrew.

"Open a Roth IRA and make monthly deposits of at least one hundred dollars."

"My parents helped me set one up two weeks ago, and I made my first deposit of $250."

"Devise an investment strategy for your Roth IRA and other investment accounts to maximize your returns while minimizing risks."

"Working on that. When I set up the account, I selected 'moderate to high risk' for now, and I'll work on the strategy part soon."

"Don't go into debt on anything but a mortgage. Buy your car with cash, purchase a home in your twenties, track your net worth, invest in assets, avoid liabilities, build your wealth."

"On track for all of that," said Andrew.

"Last but not least," said Mr. Sharp, turning to face Andrew. "Remember the first point: 'Pursue happiness.' Don't get so caught up in your financial life that you forget to have fun. You're sixteen years old. Go out on dates, stay up late with friends, enjoy the movies, blow off school occasionally—"

"You're starting to go all *Ferris Bueller's Day Off* on me," said Andrew.

"Well Ferris was on to something. What was it he said? 'Life moves pretty fast. If you don't stop and look around once in a while, you could miss it.' It's important to plan out your financial future, but it is also important to enjoy the present. That's my final point: 'Find Your Balance.'"

"Find my balance," Andrew said, clicking his pen and closing his notebook. "Is that it?"

"That's it," said Mr. Sharp. "You've successfully passed my class. It's been a pleasure."

"Pleasure's all mine," Andrew said, extending his hand. "Seriously, Mr. Sharp, I can't thank you enough. I have a feeling that your teaching has truly changed the outcome of my life, and I know I can't say that for many of my classes."

"I appreciate that, Andrew. At some point I'd like to entertain the idea of an advanced class if you'd be up for it."

"Of course!" said Andrew.

"In that case, until our paths cross again, I wish you the best, and I hope that you will also choose to pass the knowledge on to others to help them in the same way."

Andrew finished putting his notebook into his backpack and headed toward the door.

"Oh, Andrew?" Mr. Sharp asked. "I almost forgot. What are you going to do with the money?"

"The money?"

"The incentive from your father. A thousand dollars, if I remember correctly."

"Oh, that," said Andrew, smiling. "I'm thinking about working on some landscaping."

"Landscaping?" Mr. Sharp asked with a confused expression.

"Yeah," said Andrew, "in the form of a seed tree."

This Book is Just the Beginning

Want More from Mr. Sharp?

Then check out the online classes from The Seed Tree Group (www.seedtreegroup.com) designed to help build financial literacy. Instead of the dry, boring approach to traditional classes, students enrolled in these classes will join author Stephen Carter for engaging lessons straight from the classroom of Mr. Sharp.

Since you are a valued reader of the book, you are entitled to receive 30% off the purchase price of any of the classes. Simply pick up your phone and take a picture of the following QR code to receive your coupon:

In the end, your financial future is up to you. By starting today, you are ensuring a head start that will reap enormous benefits down the road.

Recommended Reading List (Based on Concepts Introduced in This Book)

1. *Atomic Habits* by James Clear
2. *The Slight Edge: Secret to a Successful Life* by Jeff Olson
3. *The Millionaire Next Door: The Surprising Secrets of America's Wealthy* by Thomas J. Stanley and William D. Danko
4. *The 7 Habits of Highly Effective People* by Stephen R. Covey
5. *The Magic of Thinking Big* by David Schwartz
6. *Start with Why* by Simon Sinek
7. *The Automatic Millionaire* by David Bach
8. *The 12% Solution* by David Alan Carter
9. *Rich Dad, Poor Dad* by Robert Kiyosaki

About the Author

After fourteen years of teaching honors and AP English, author Stephen Carter left the traditional classroom to start a brand-new entrepreneurship program at the high school where he worked. Beginning with a student-run coffee bar, the program grew into a full-scale operation complete with a developed curriculum and a string of successful businesses, all managed by students in the program.

His passion is for getting students out of the classroom and into hands-on learning situations where they can develop innovative solutions to real-world problems. As the director of Entrepreneurship, Stephen also oversees the program offshoots, which include a new culinary arts department along with a horticulture department.

Because he felt the educational system as a whole lacked teaching centering on personal finance, he started The Seed Tree Group to help promote financial literacy for teens in order to help them get a jump start in life and take advantage of the time value of money. *The Seed Tree: A Financial Fable* is the first in a coming series that will convey financial concepts through the story form. He personally teaches the online classes from The Seed Tree Group and infuses them with his passion for education and personal finance.

When he isn't at the school, Stephen can be found tinkering with a recipe in the kitchen, hiking the Appalachian Trail, or looking for his next good read. He lives in Cincinnati, Ohio, with his wife, two children, and two dogs.

—

Master of Arts from Xavier University
Financial Management Certificate from Cornell University

Visit www.seedtreegroup.com to learn more.